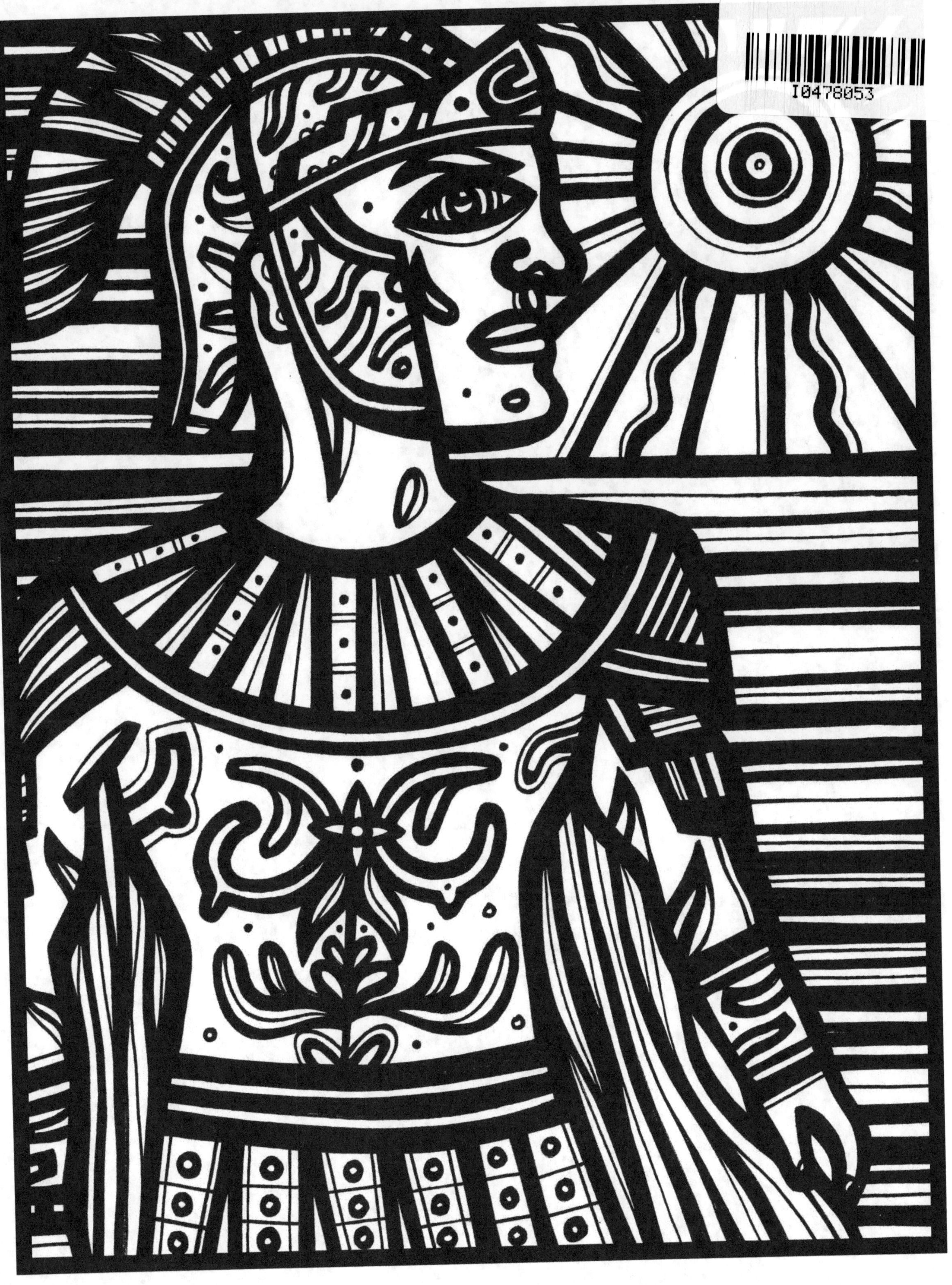

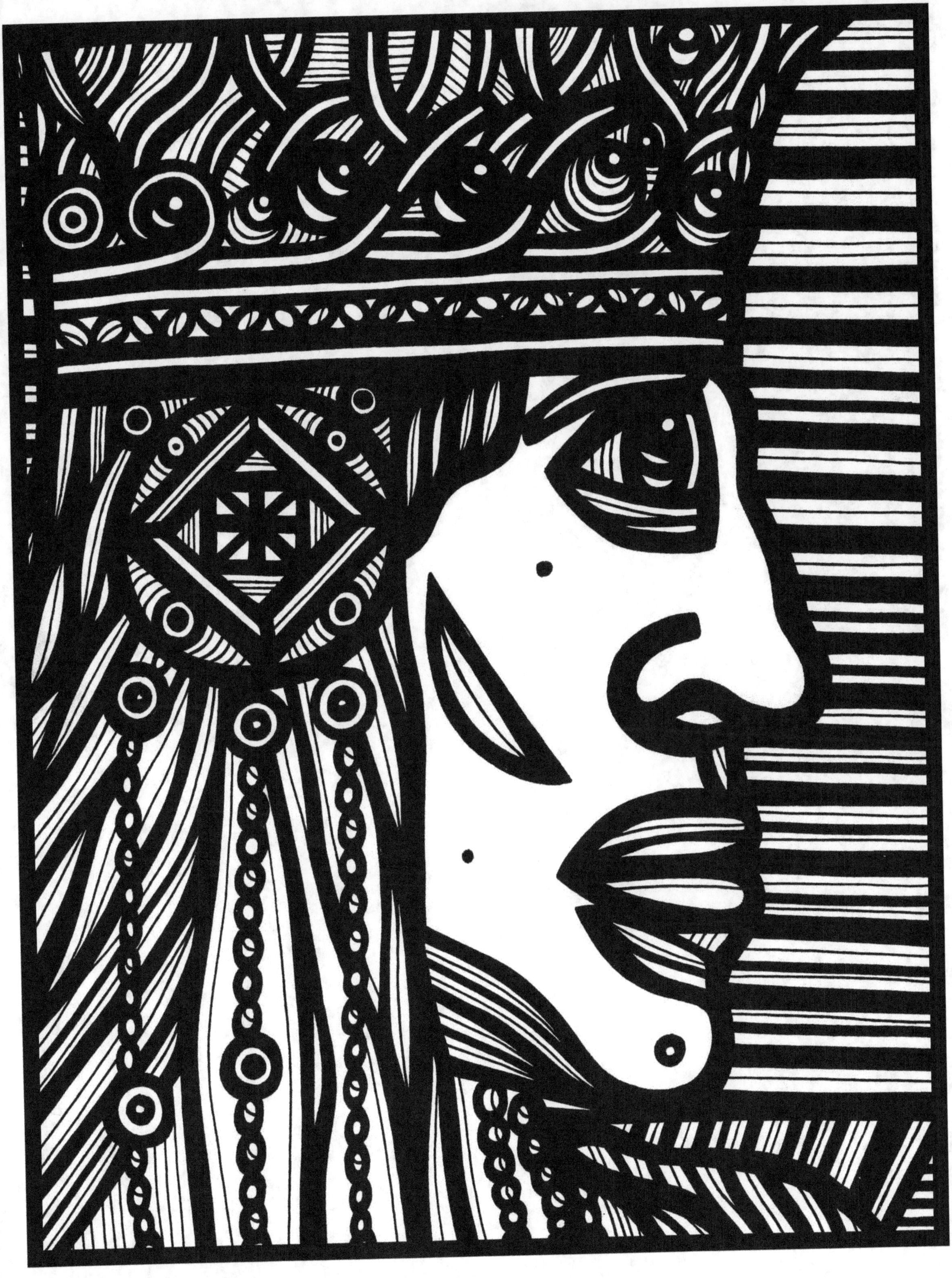

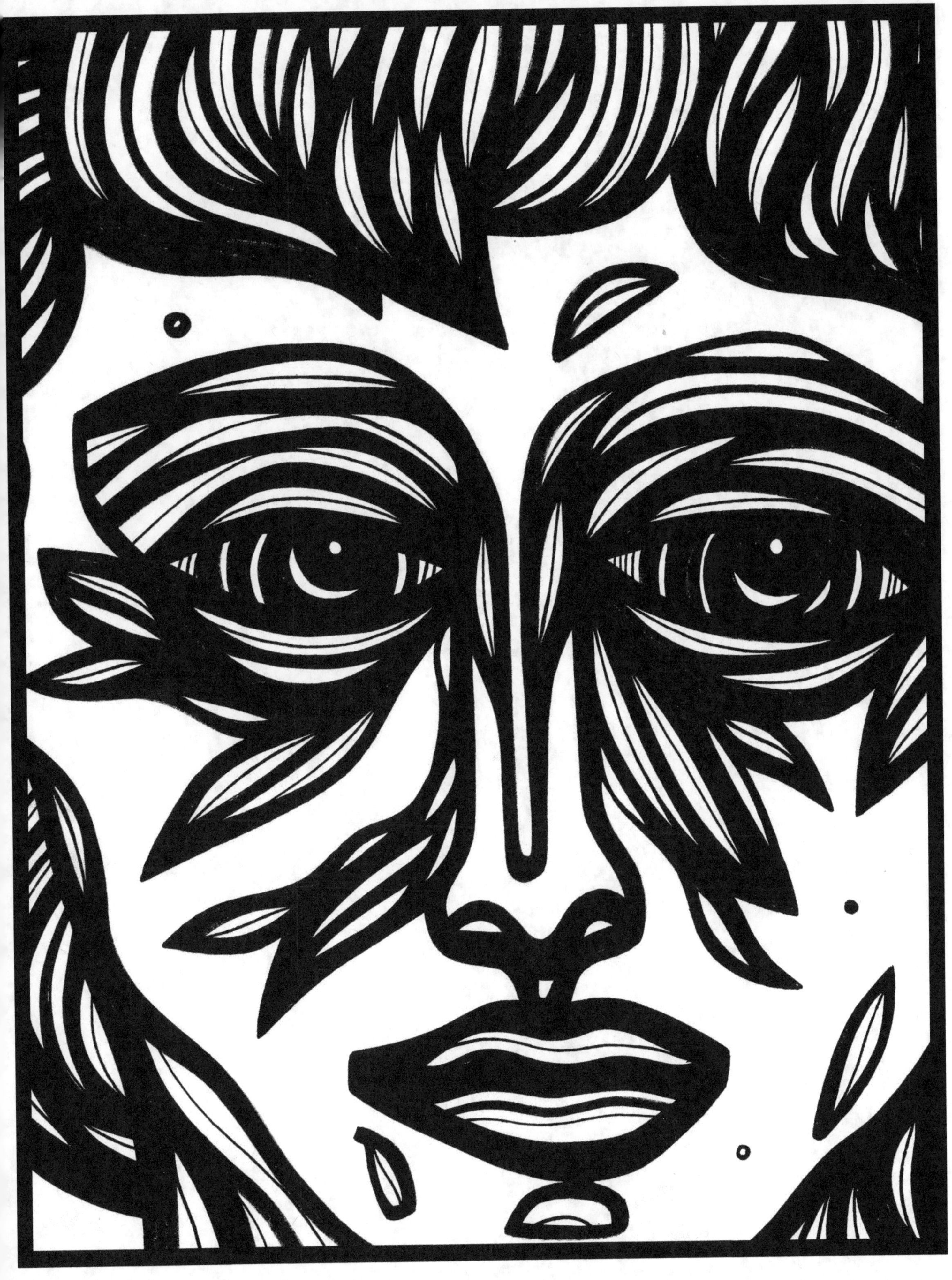

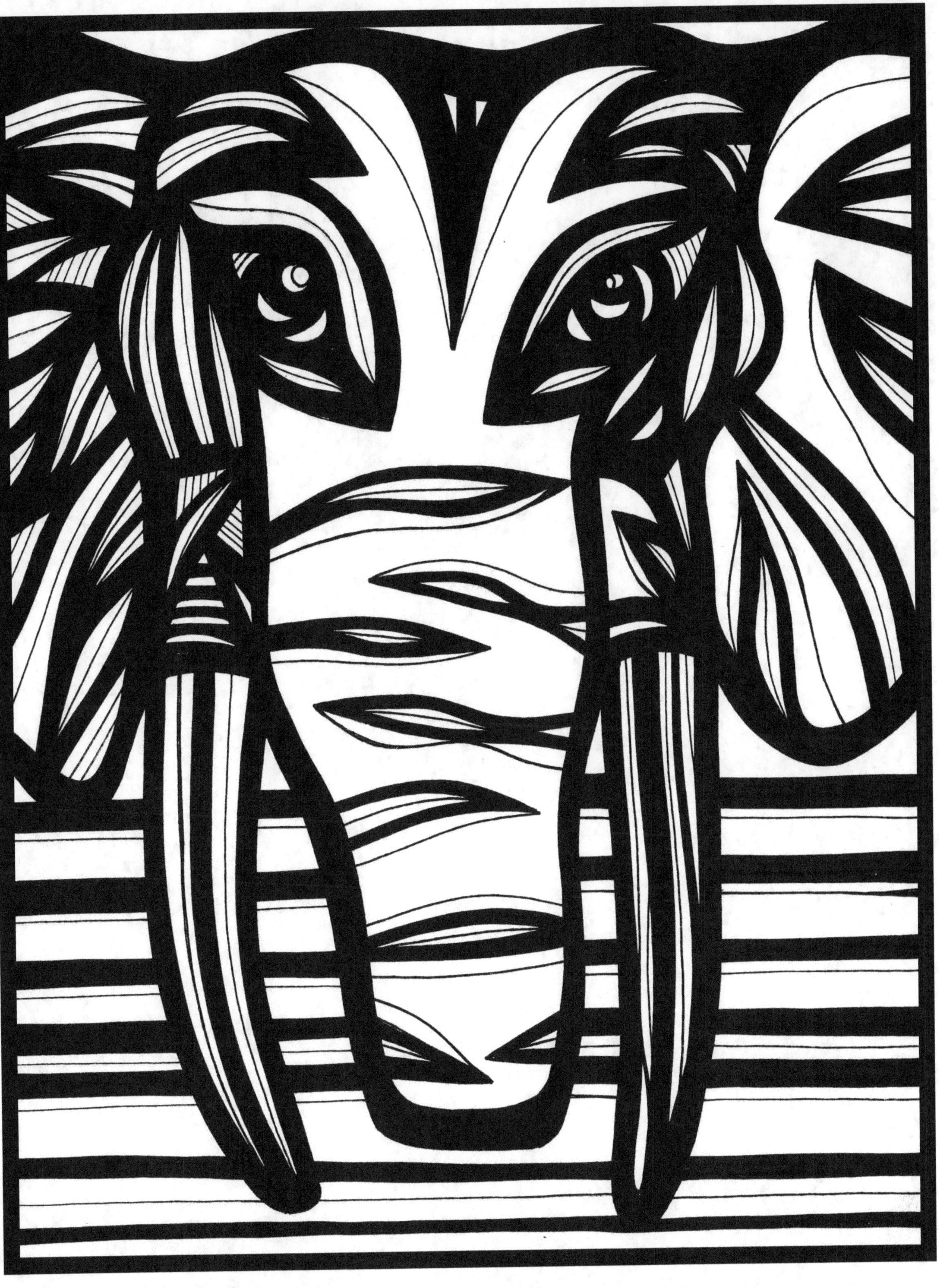

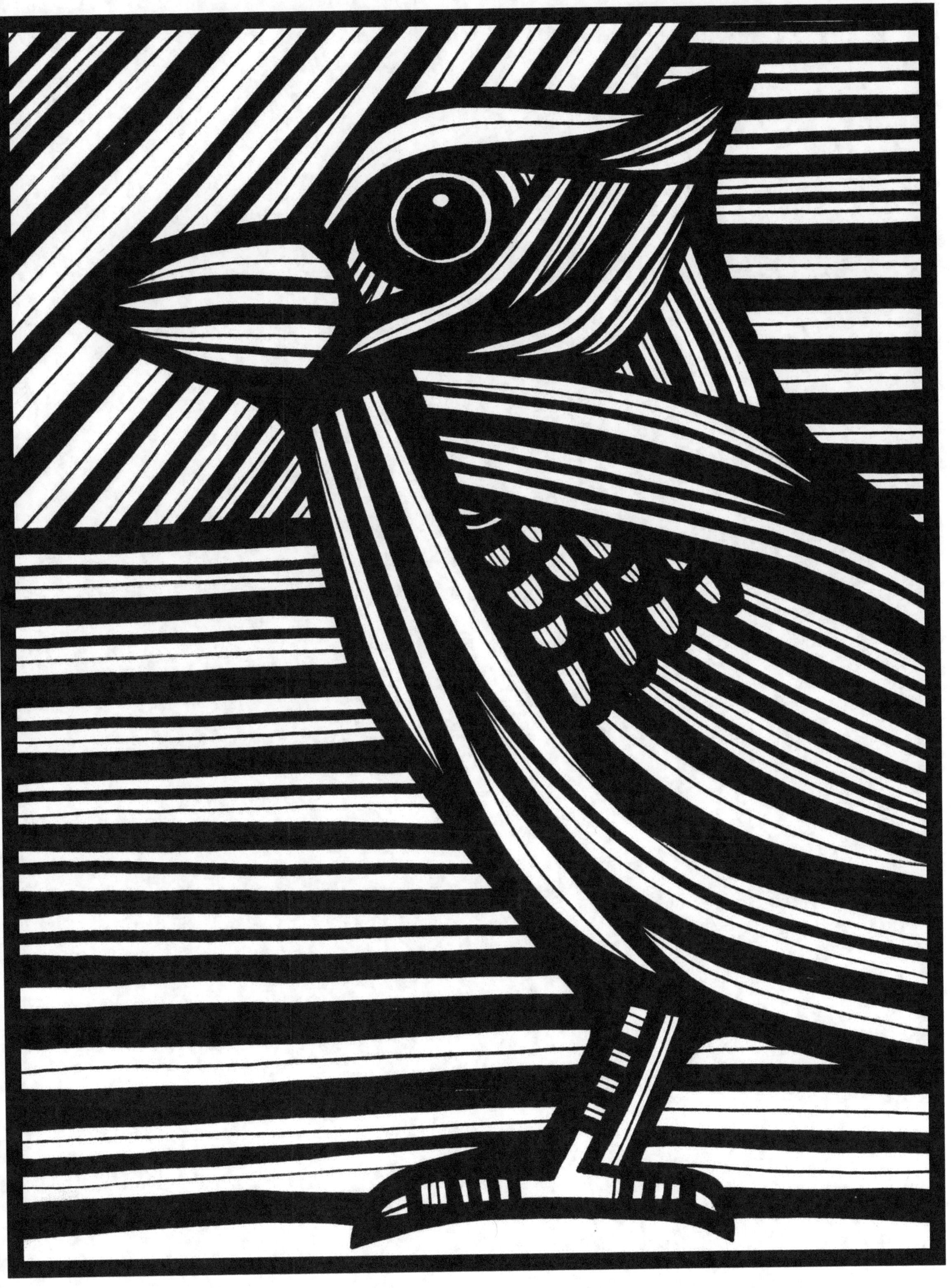

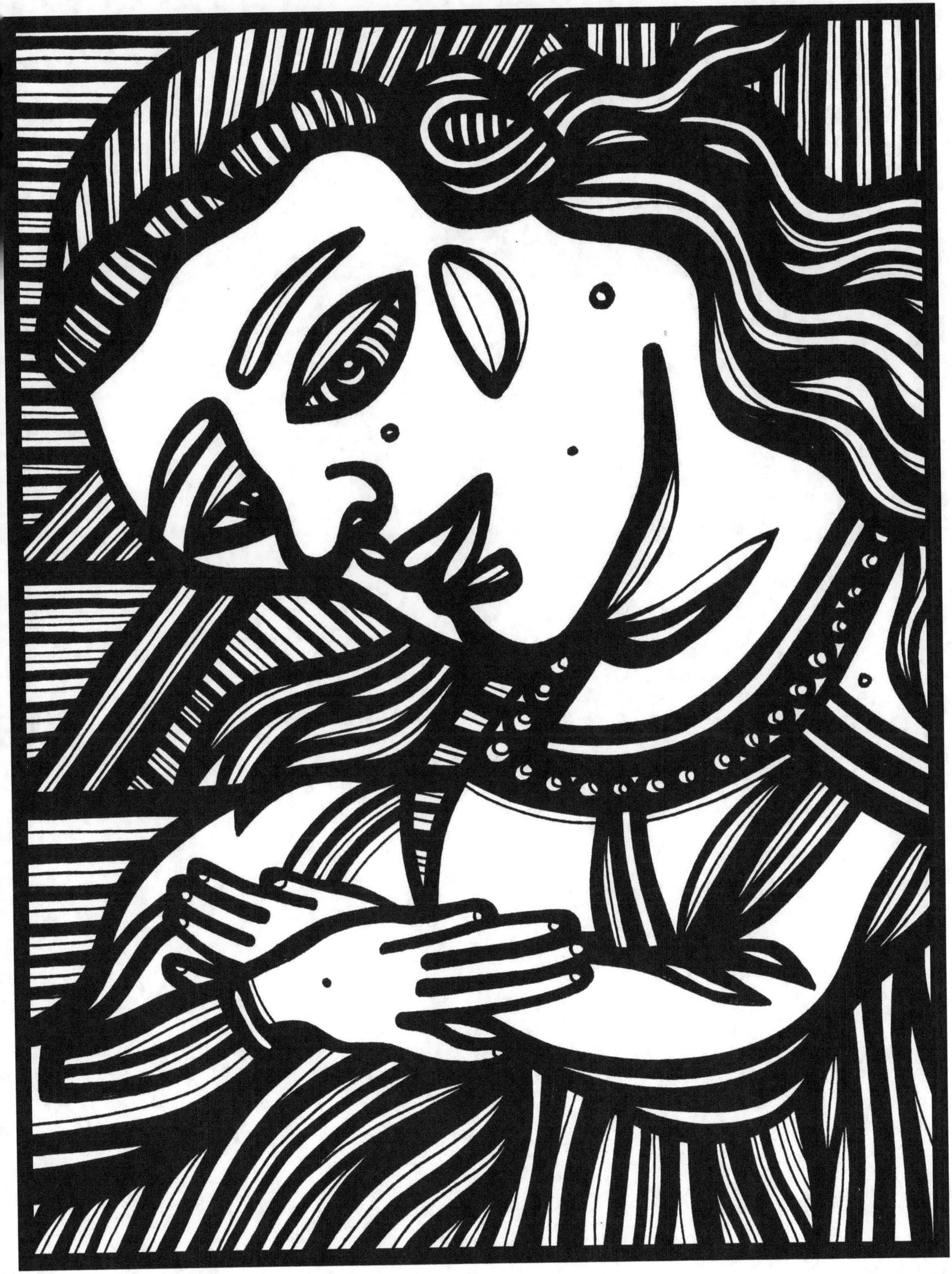

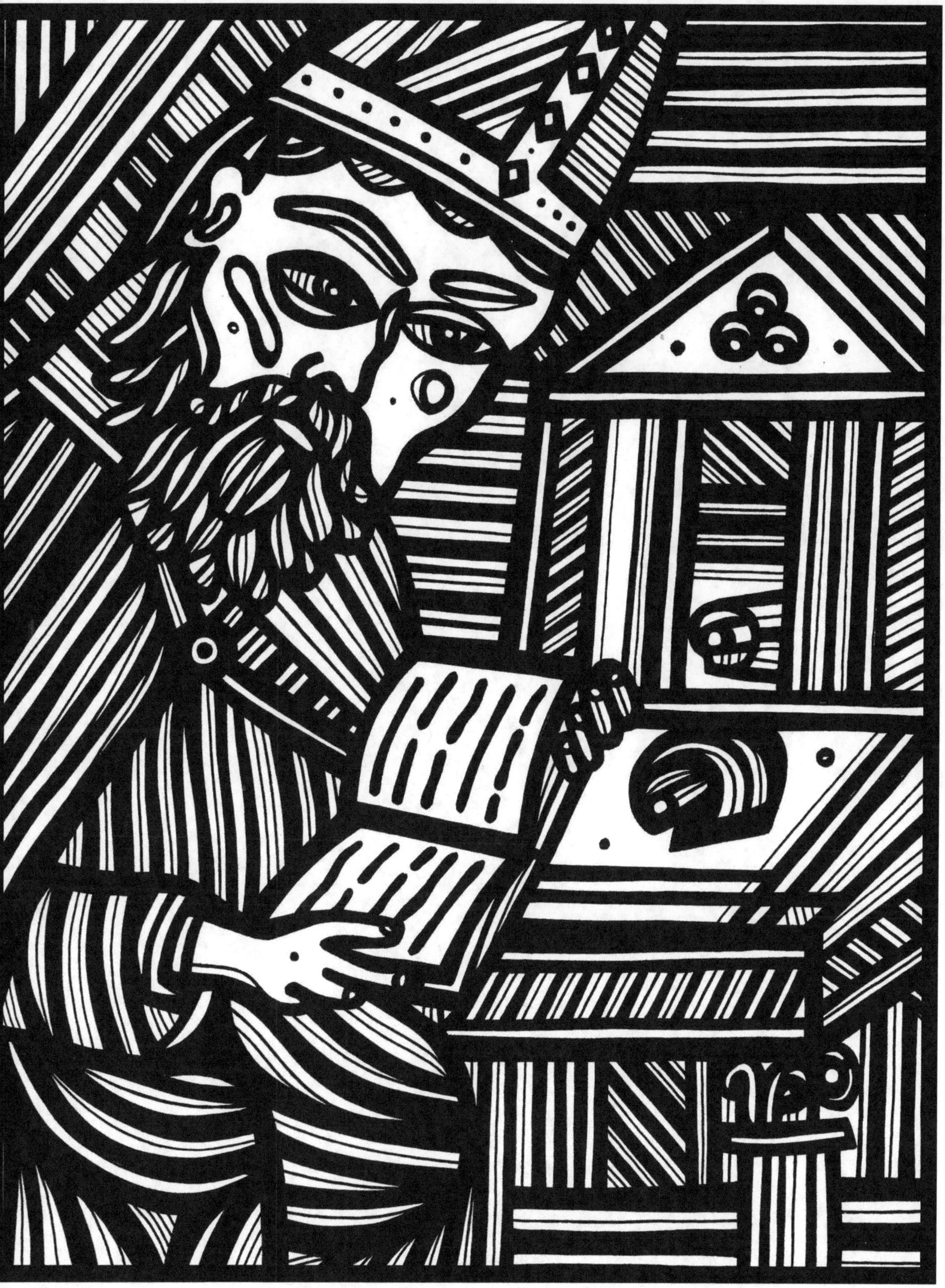

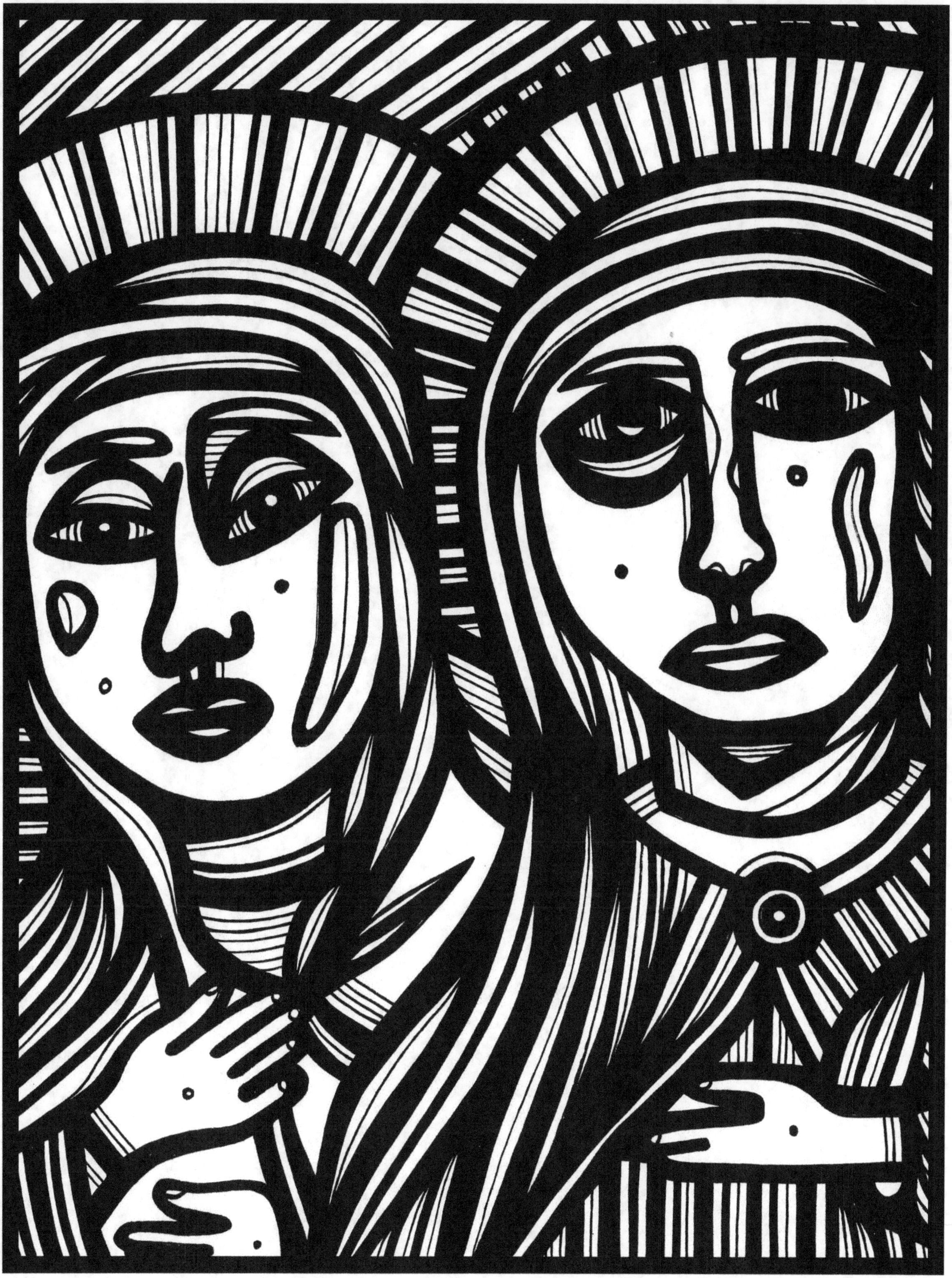

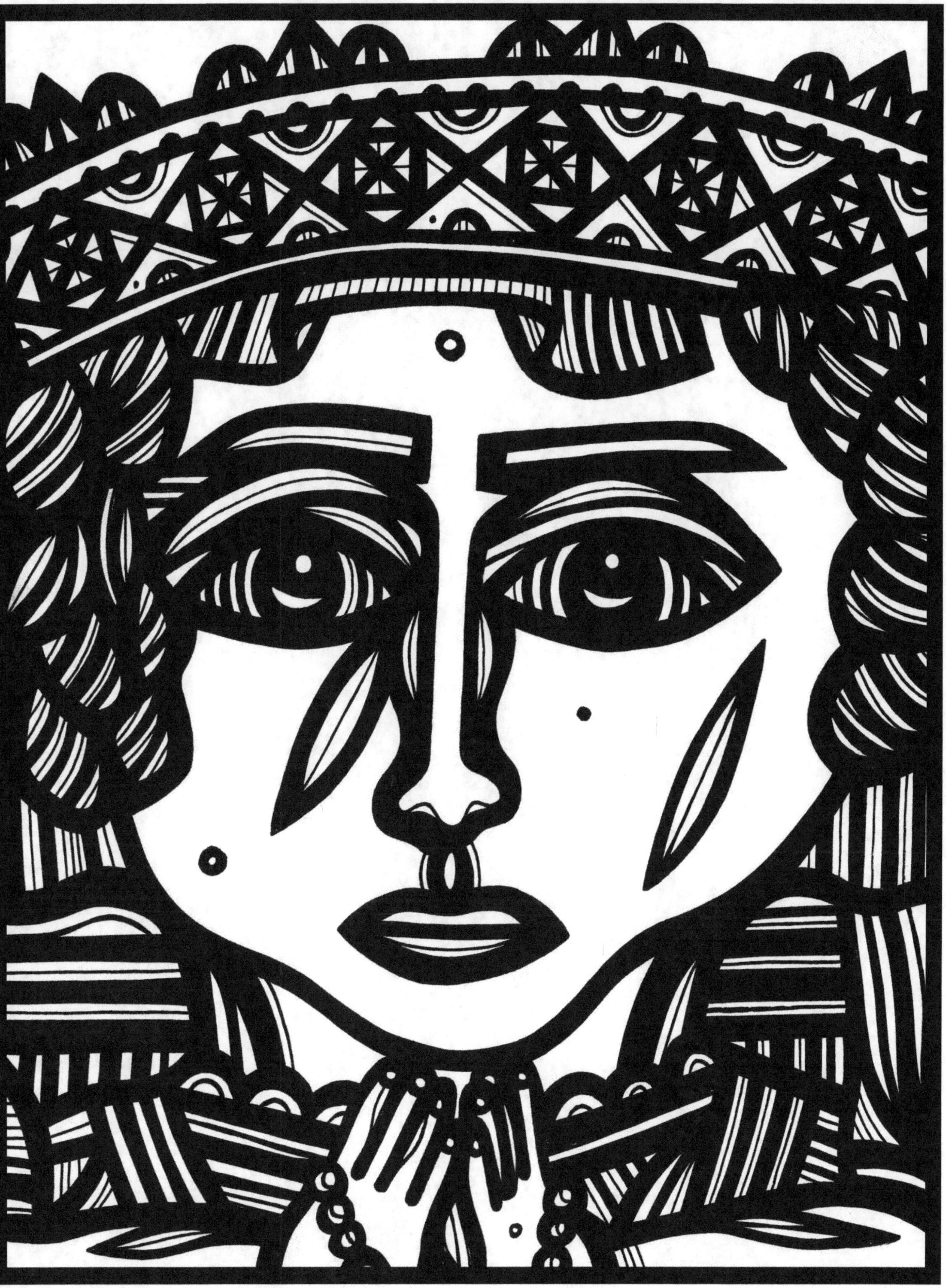

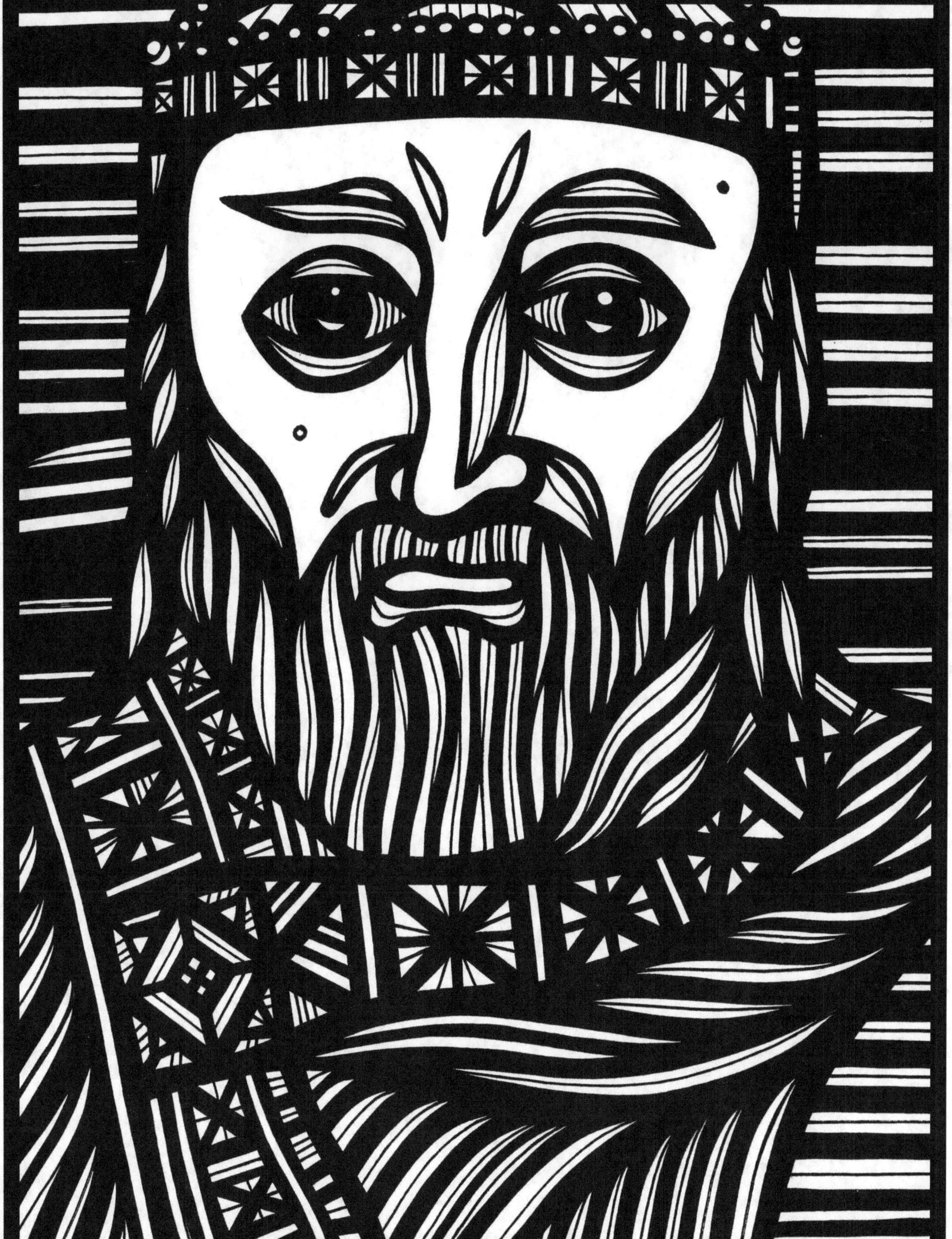

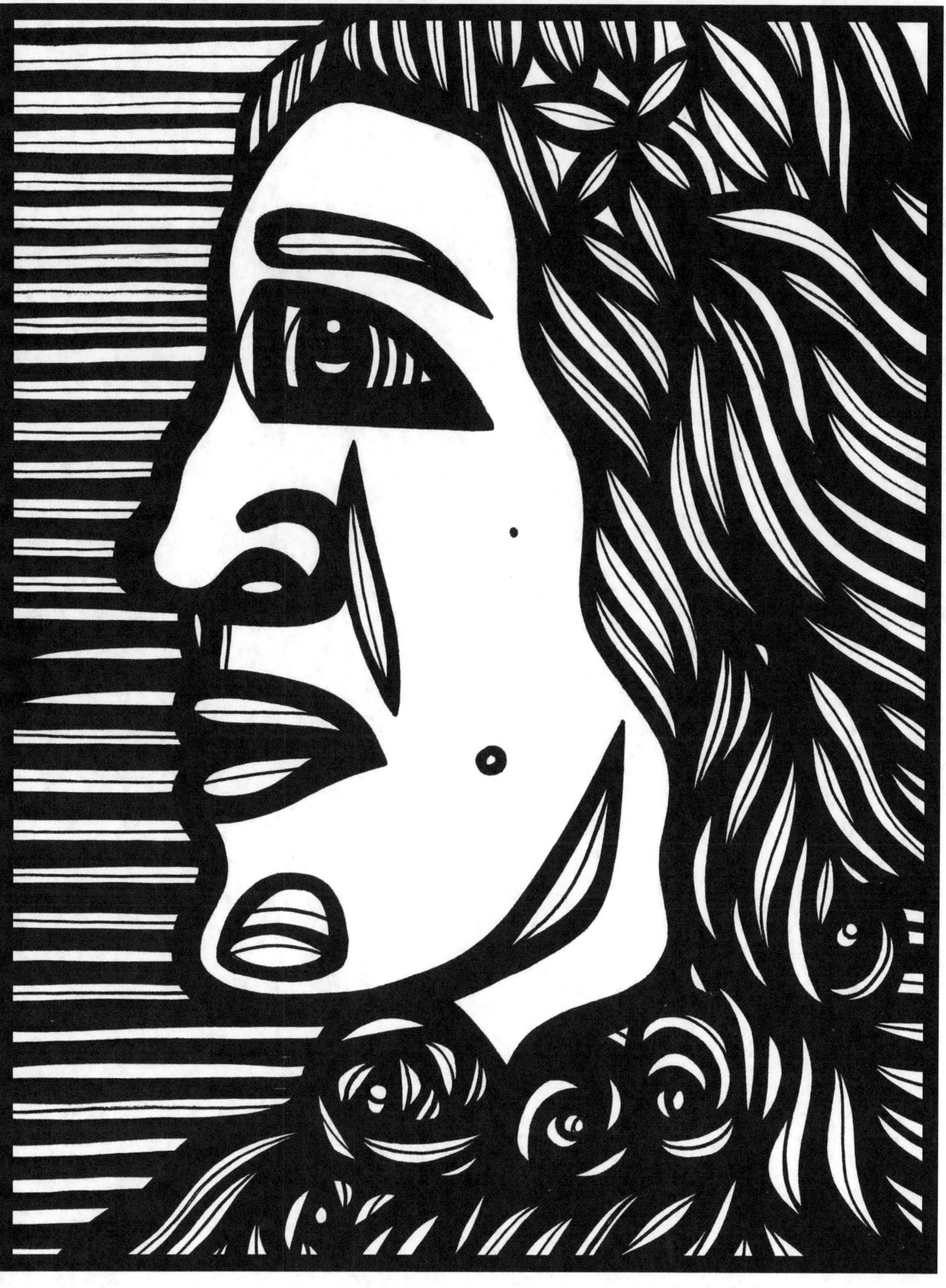

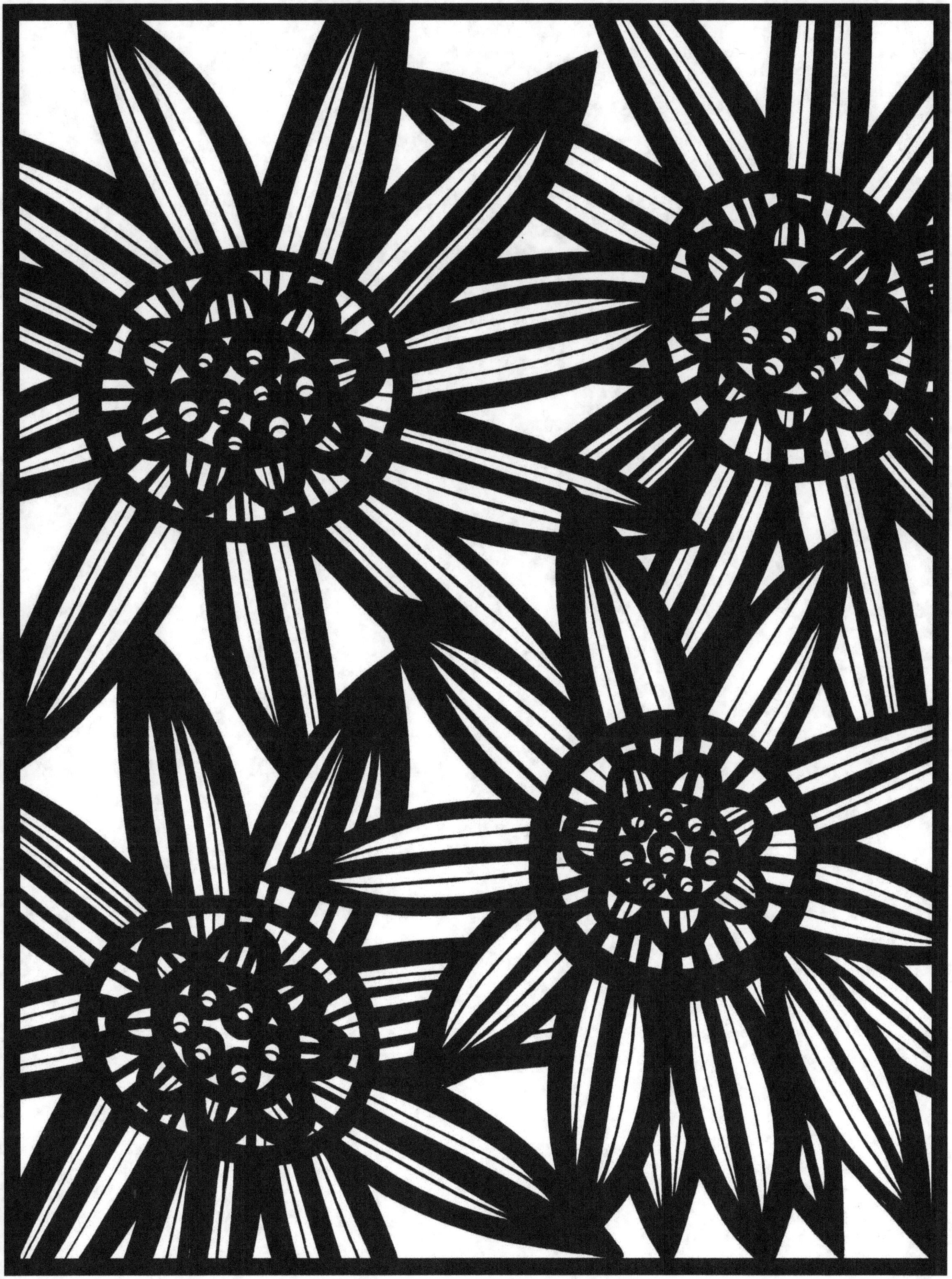

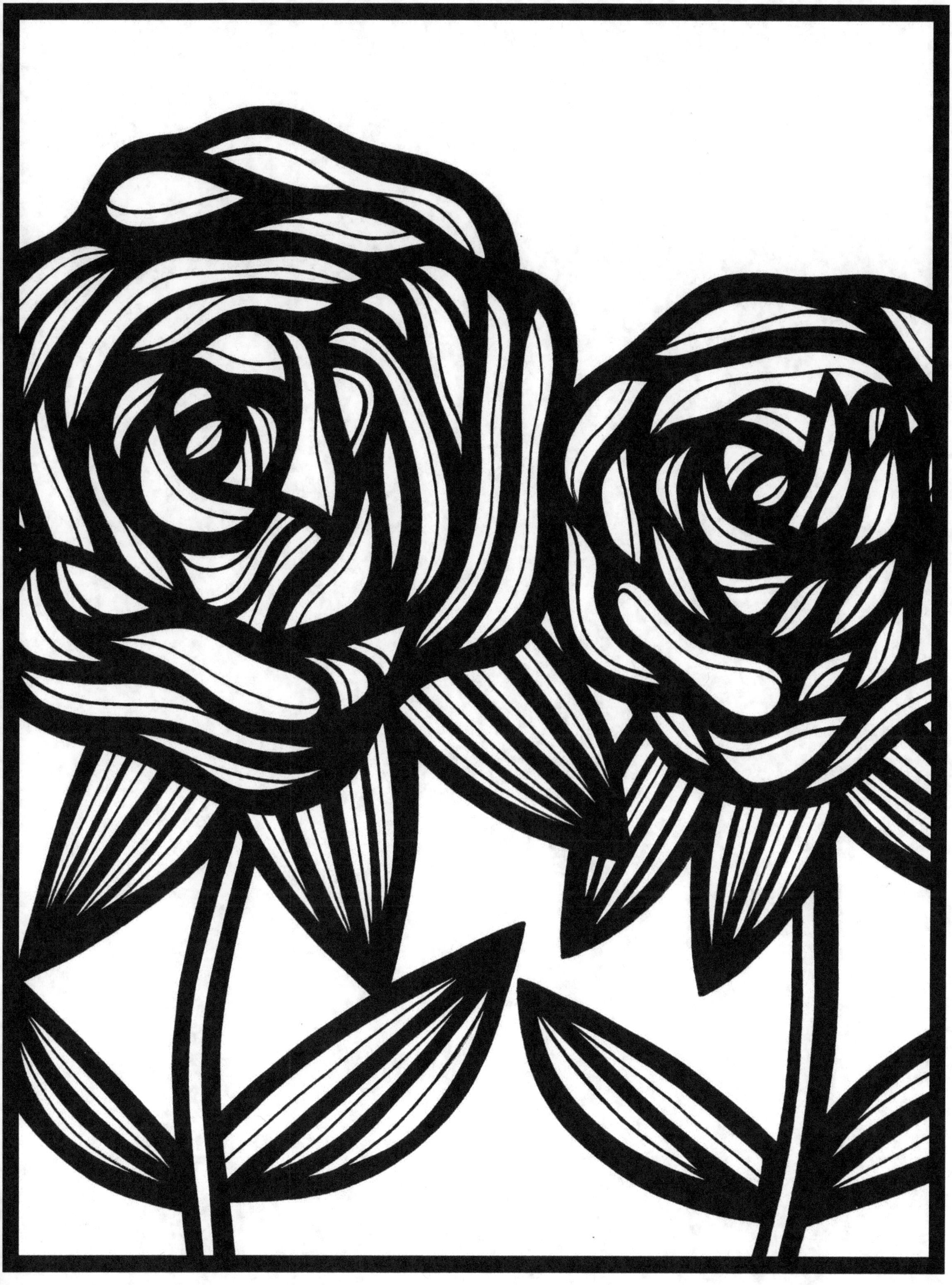

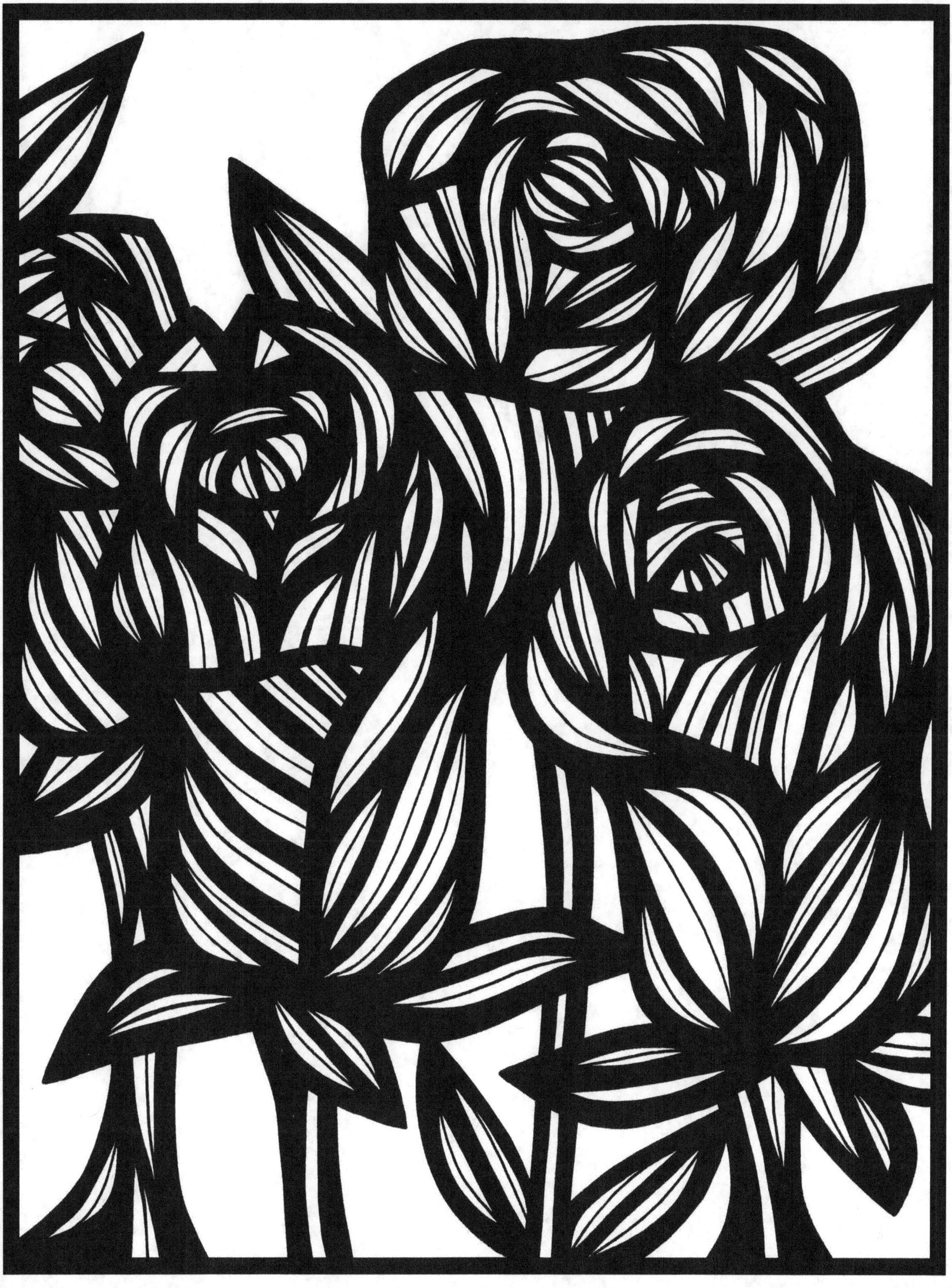

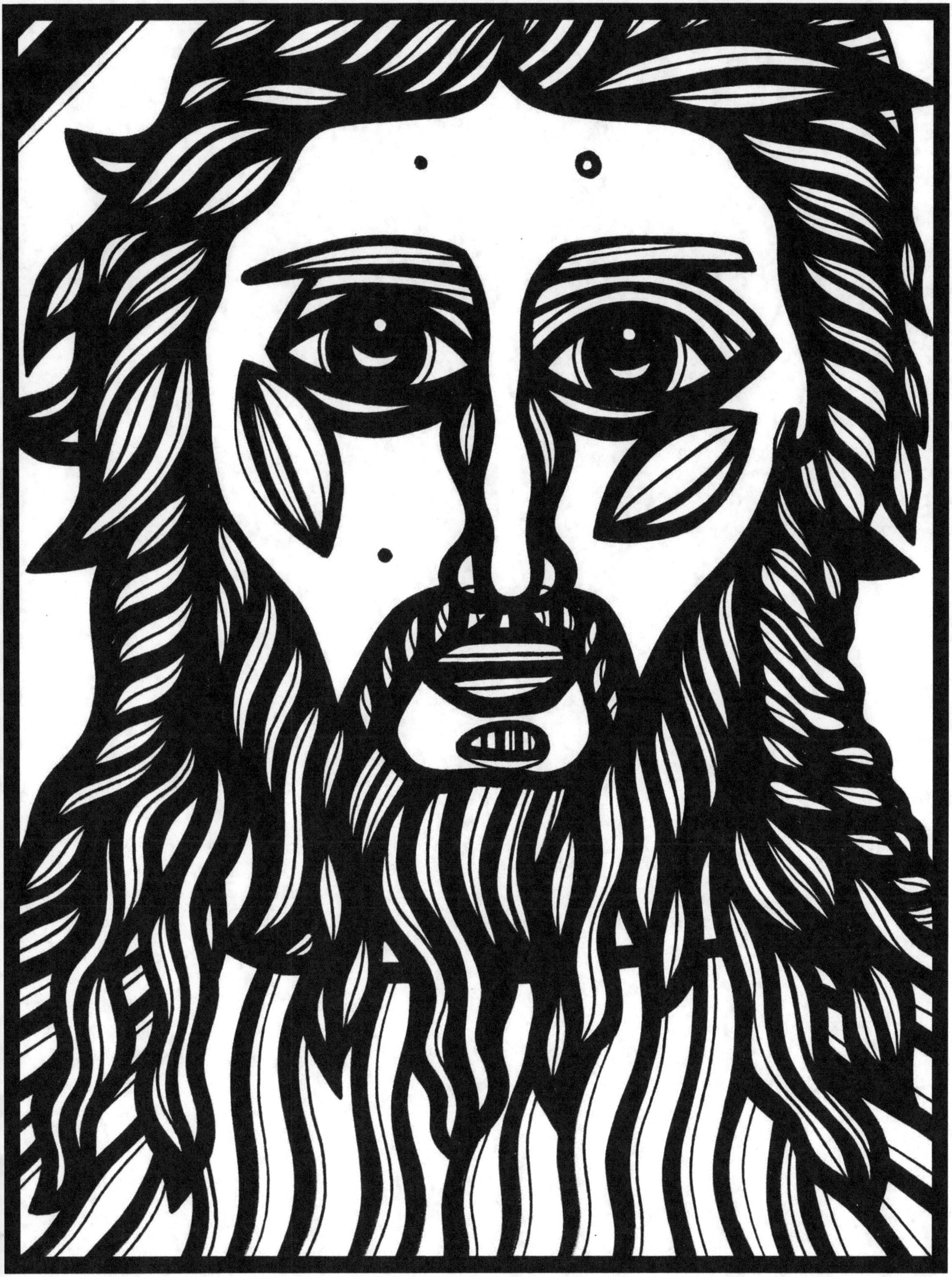

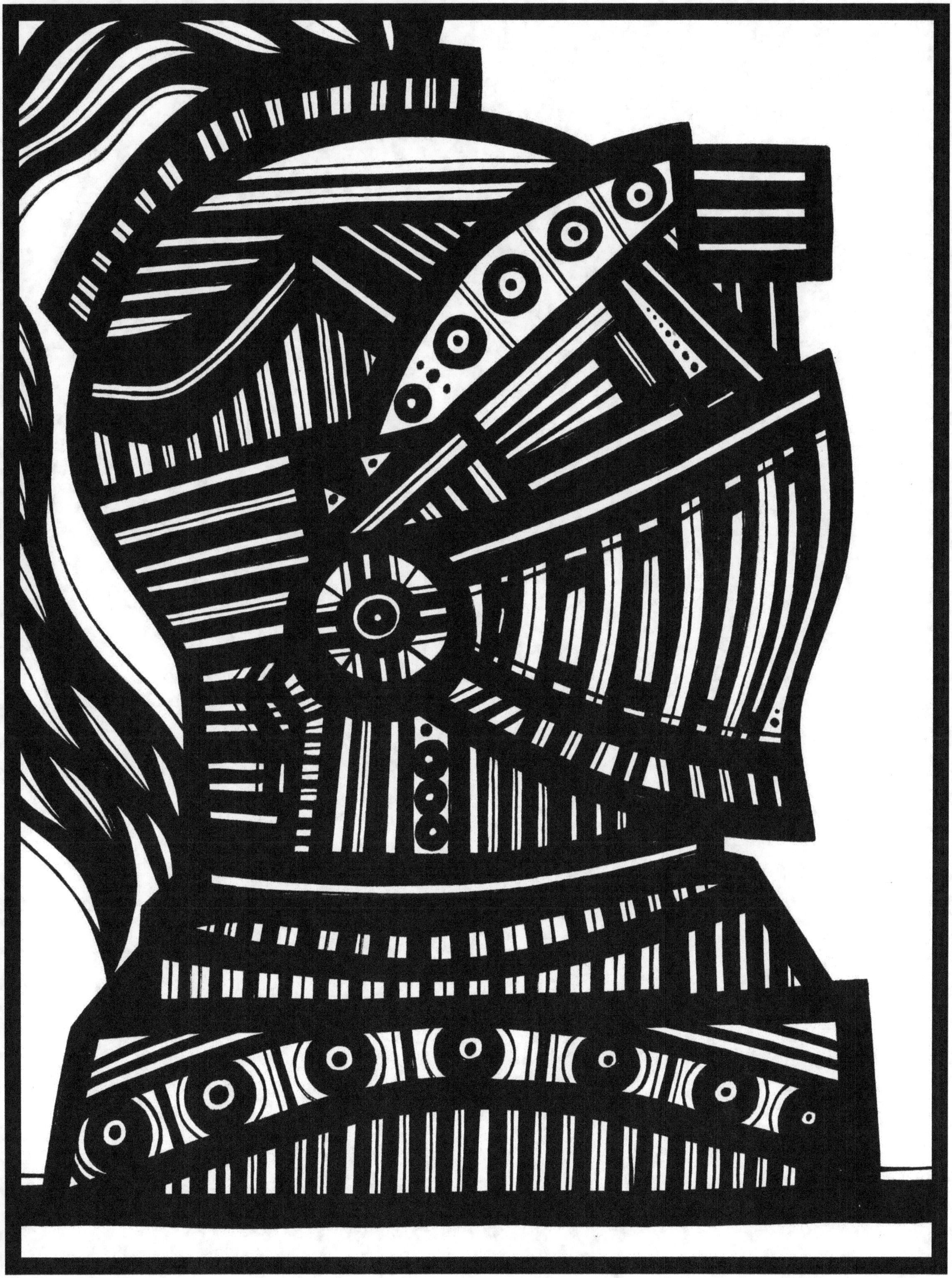

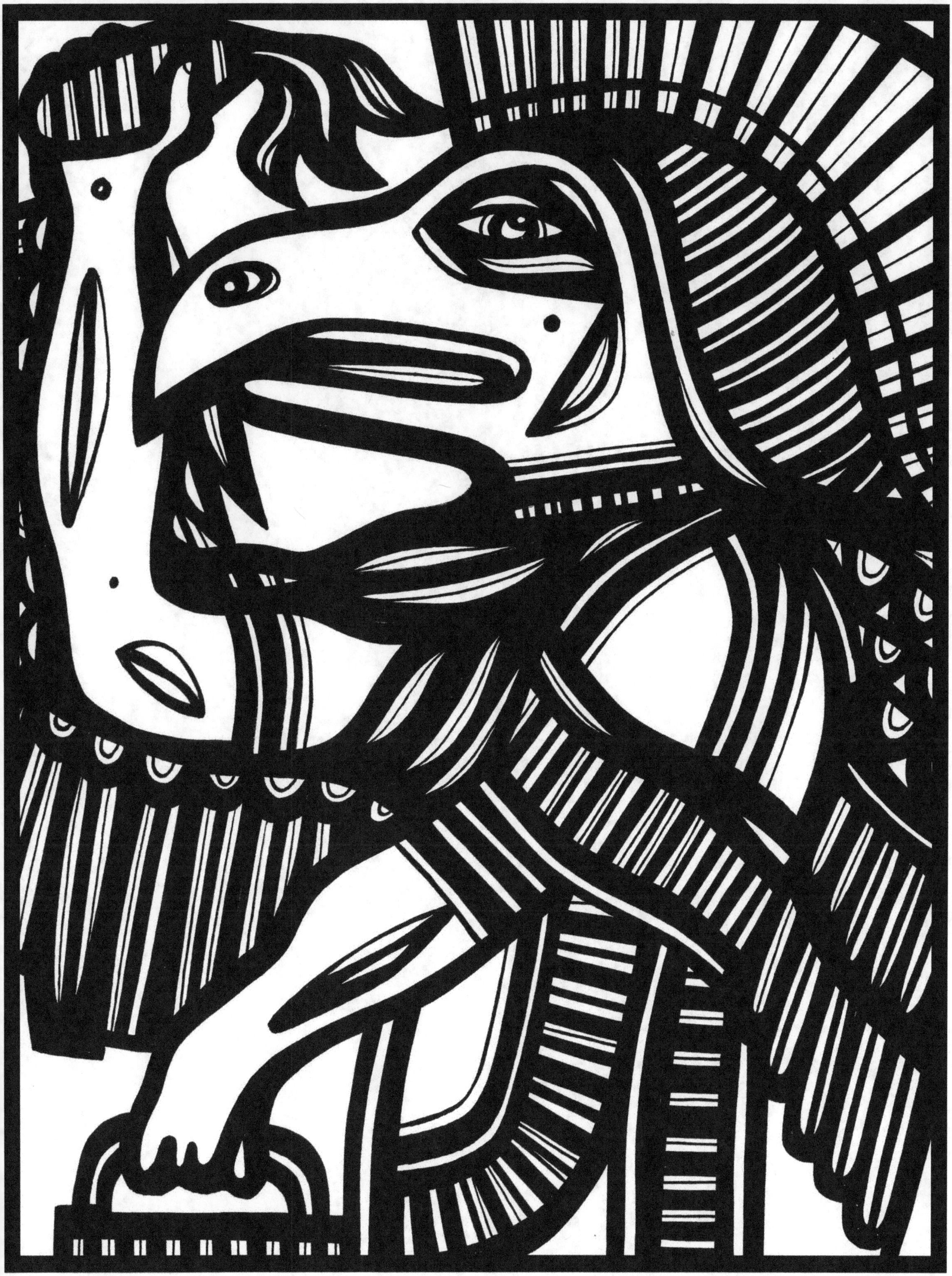

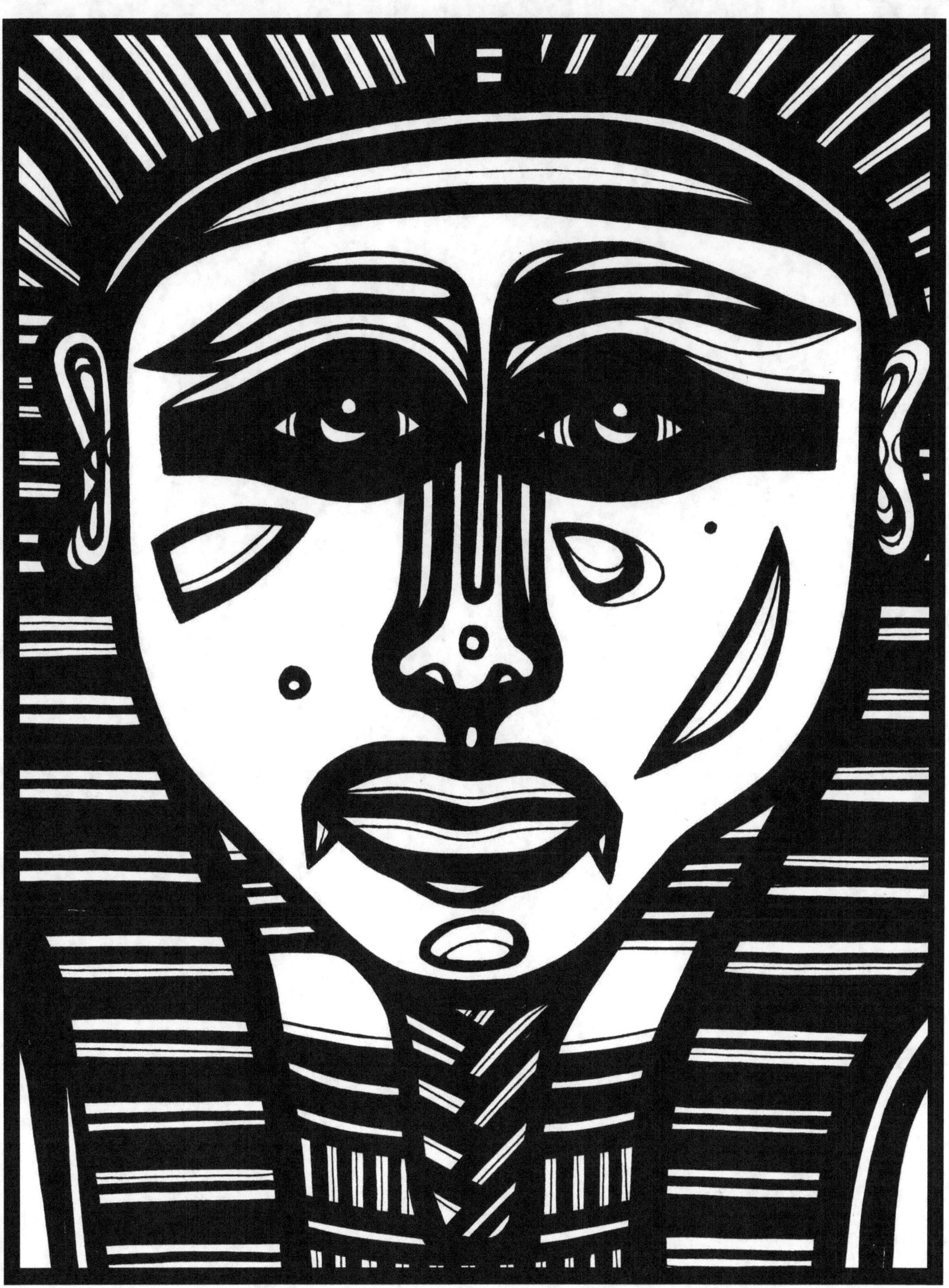

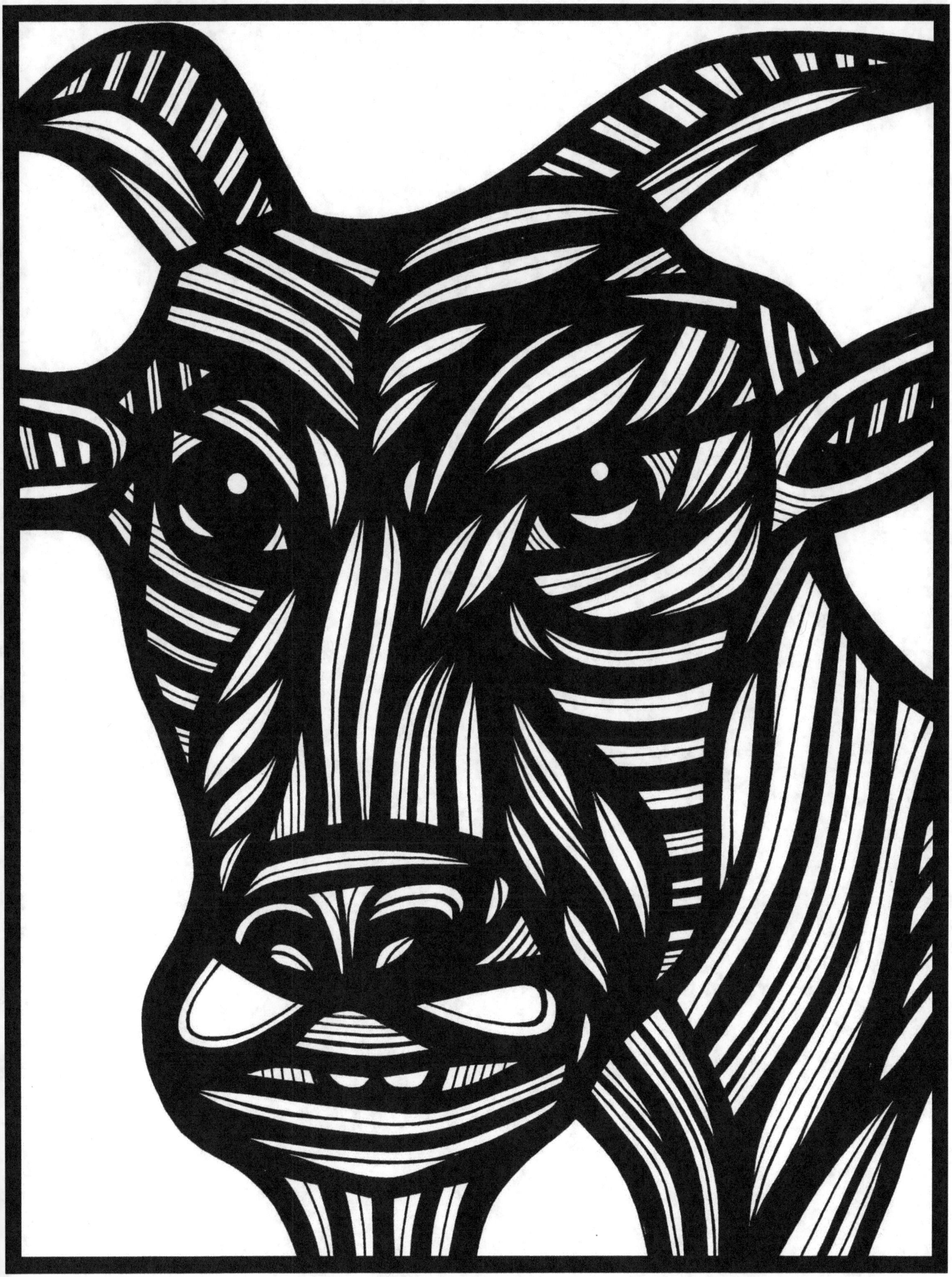

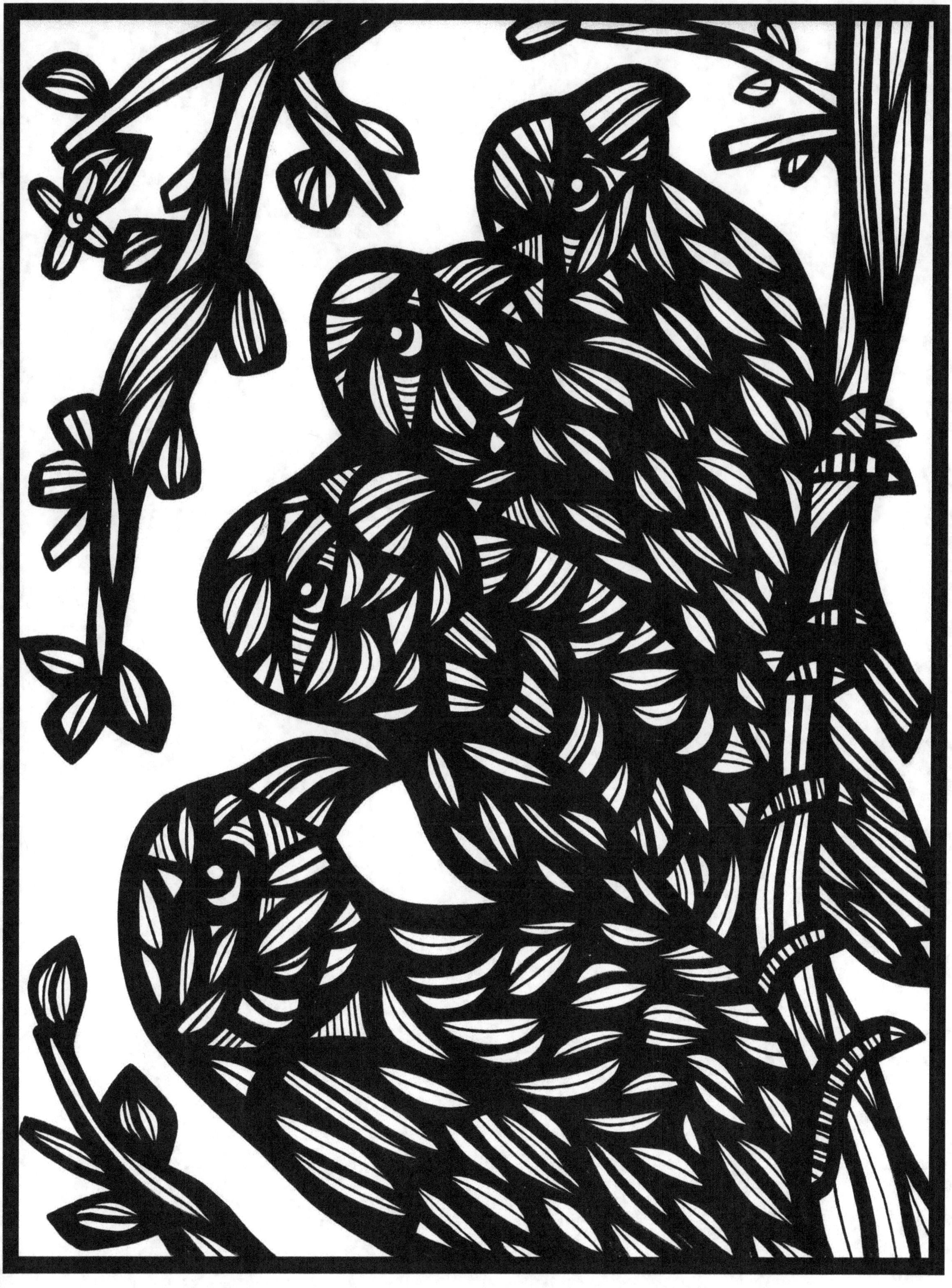

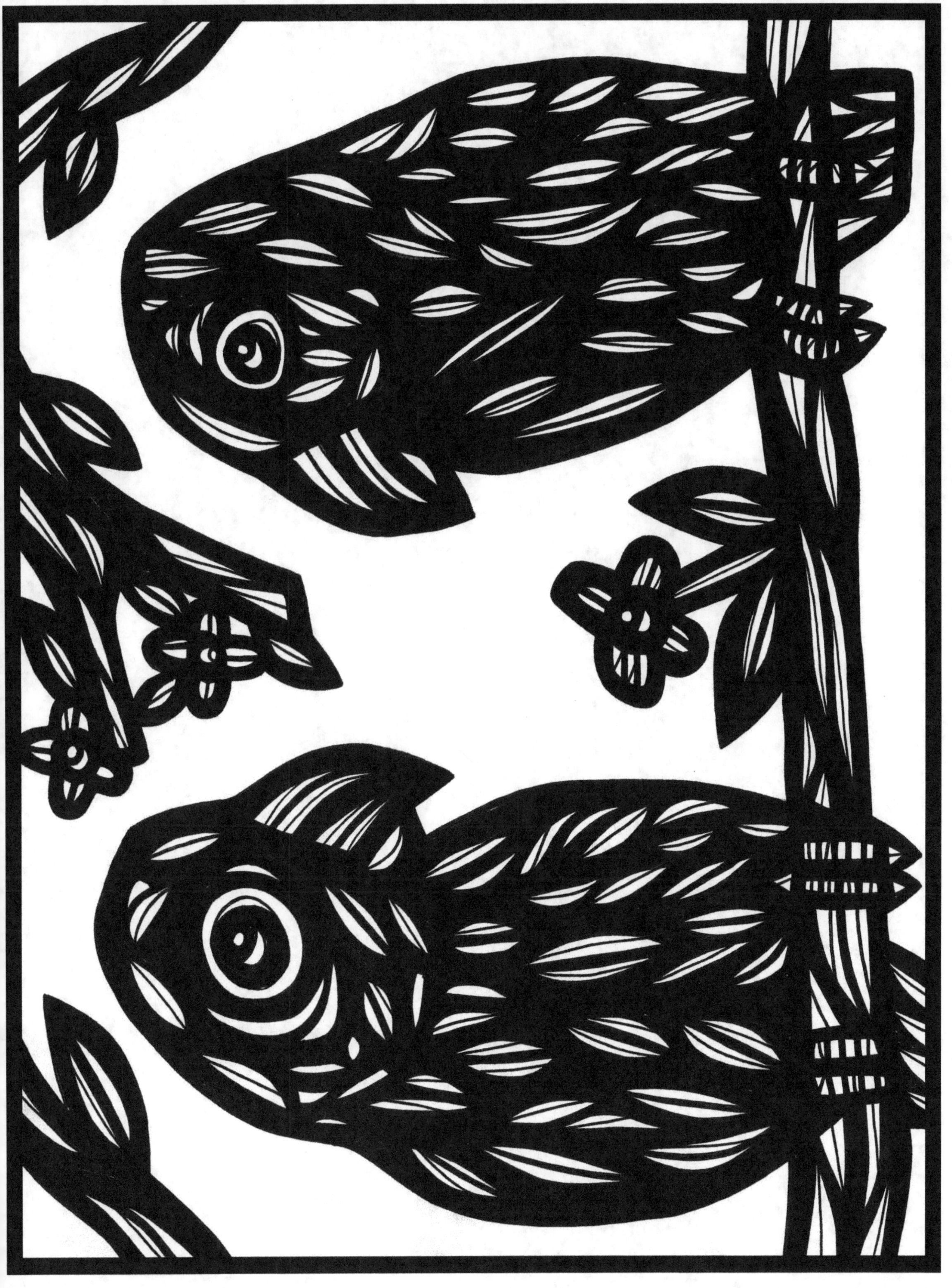

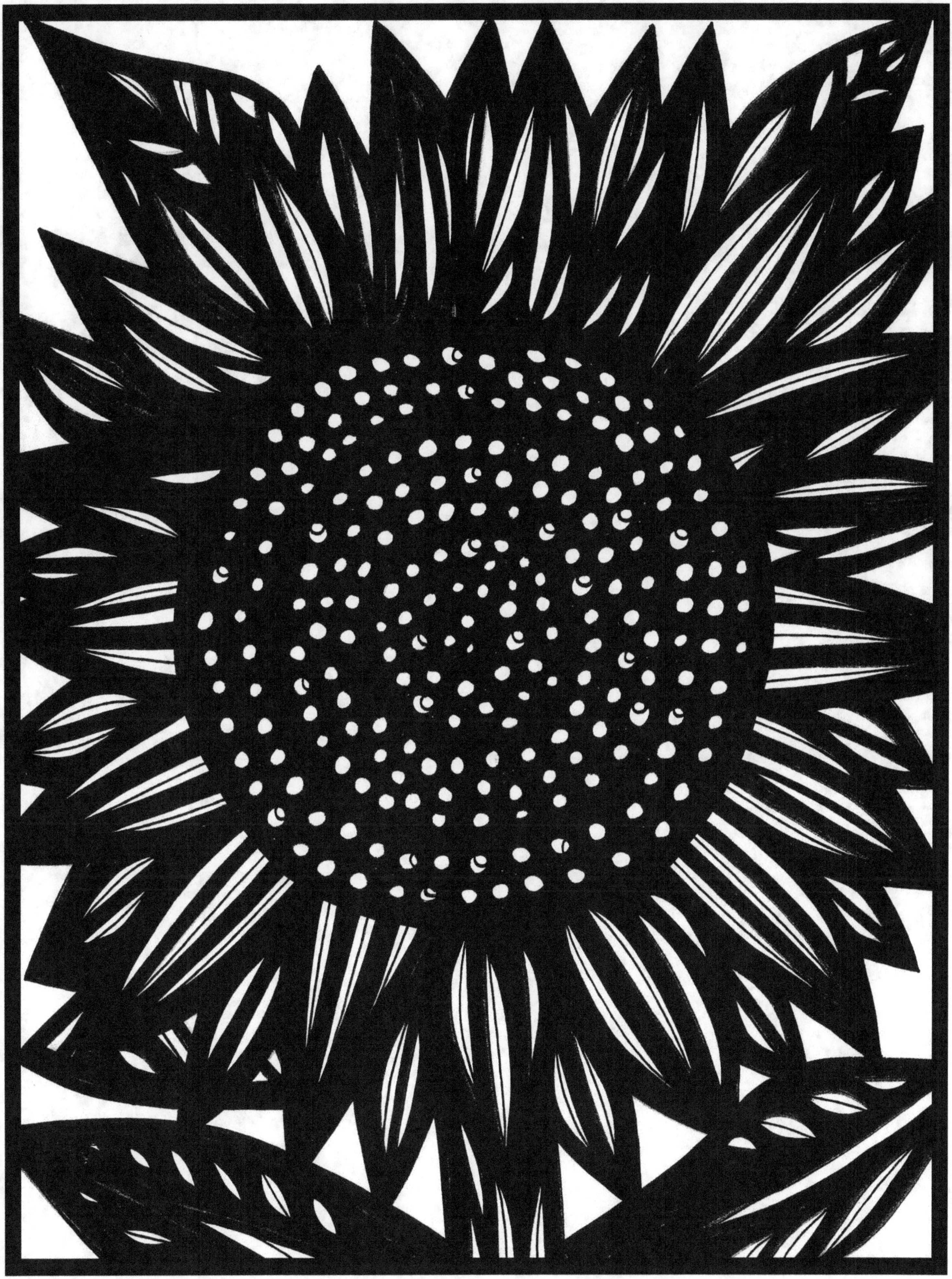

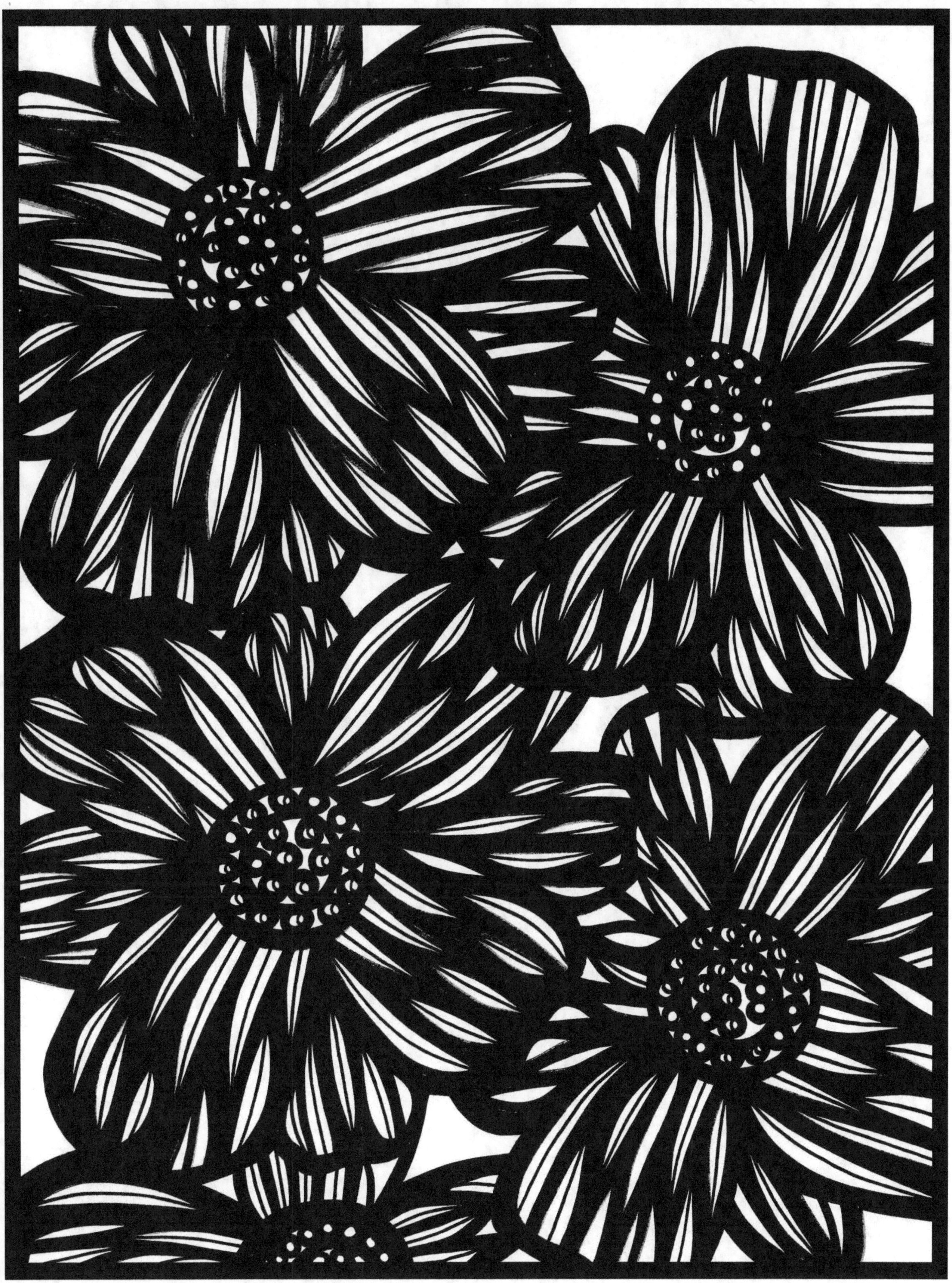

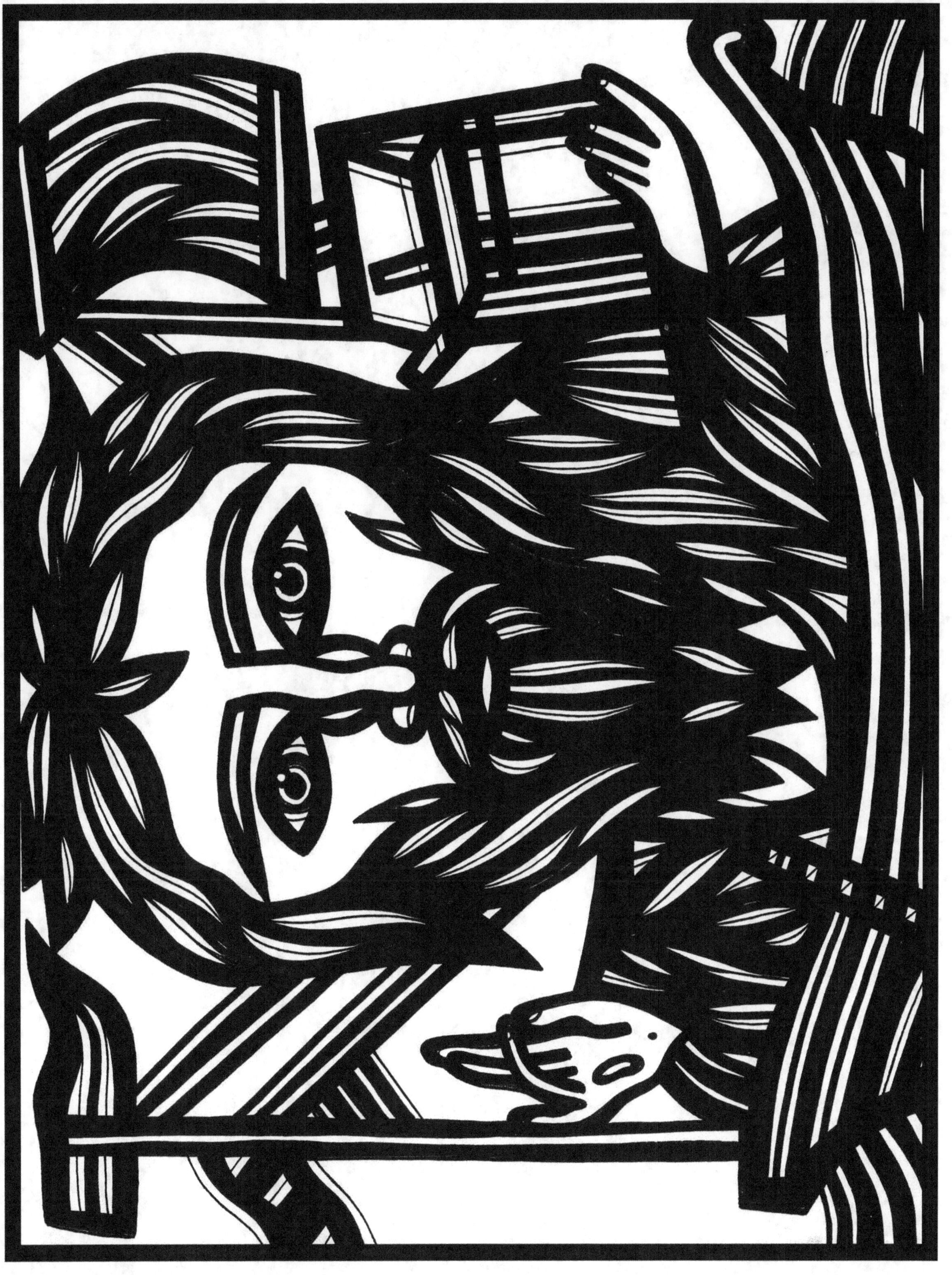

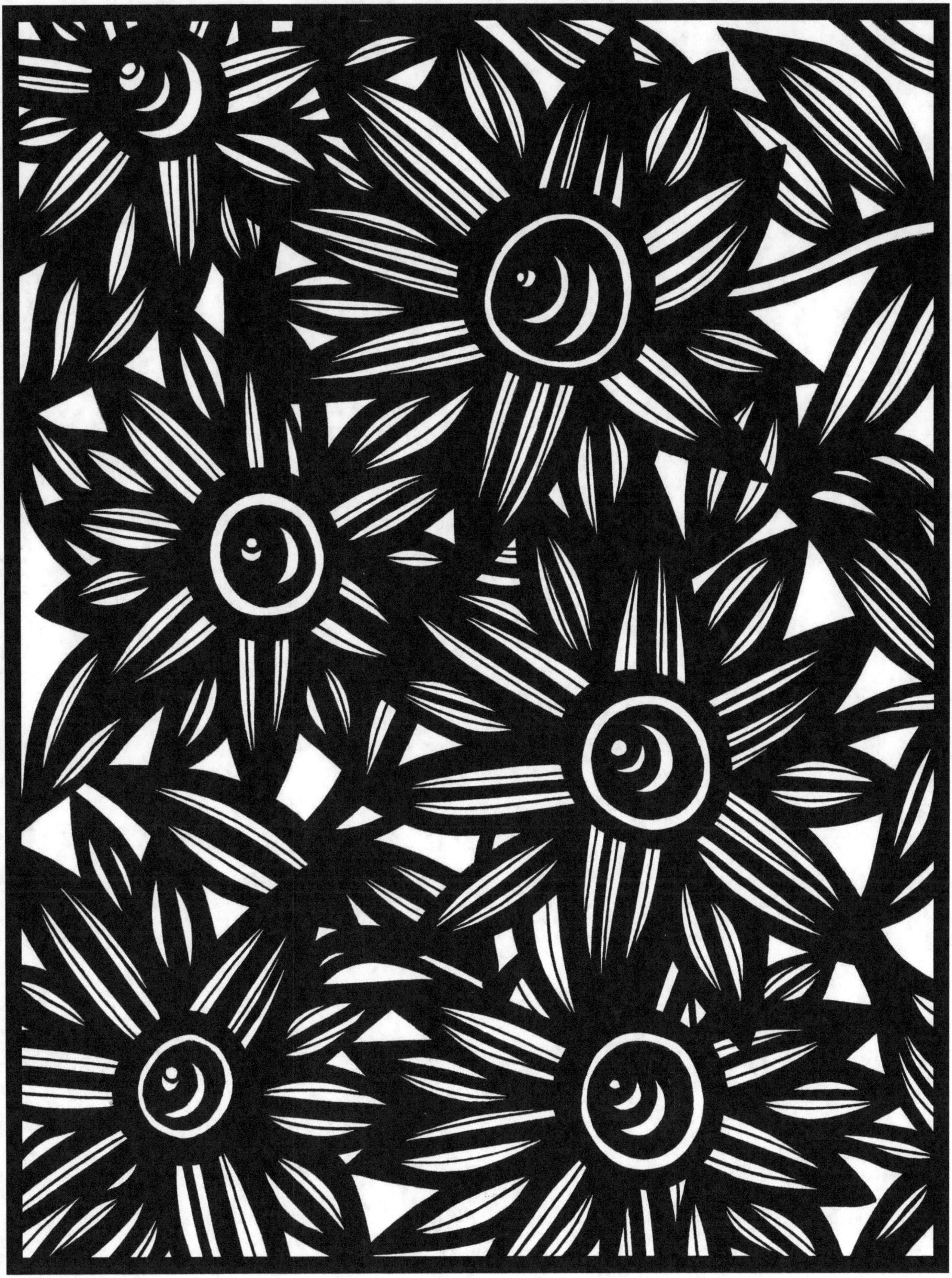

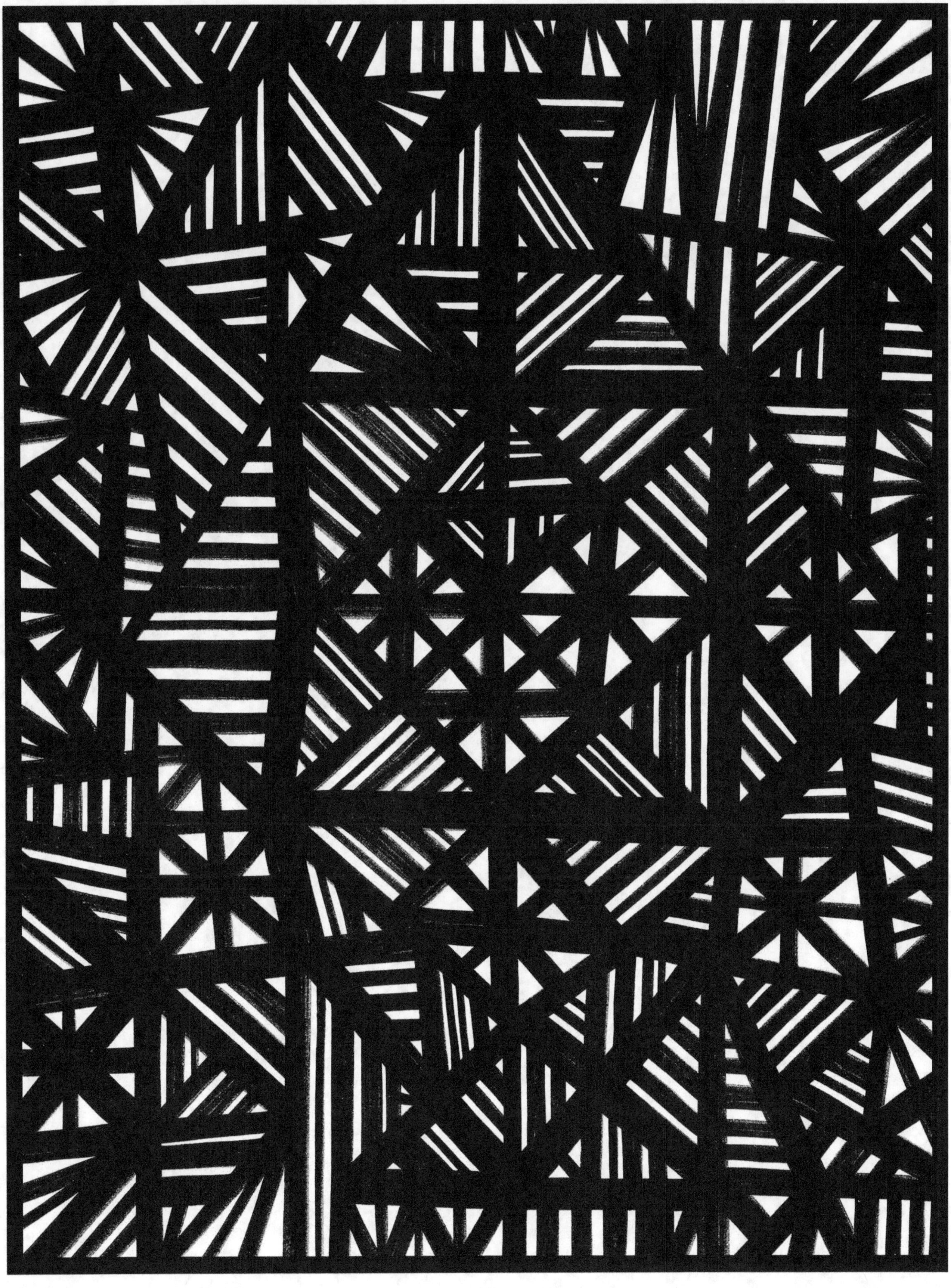

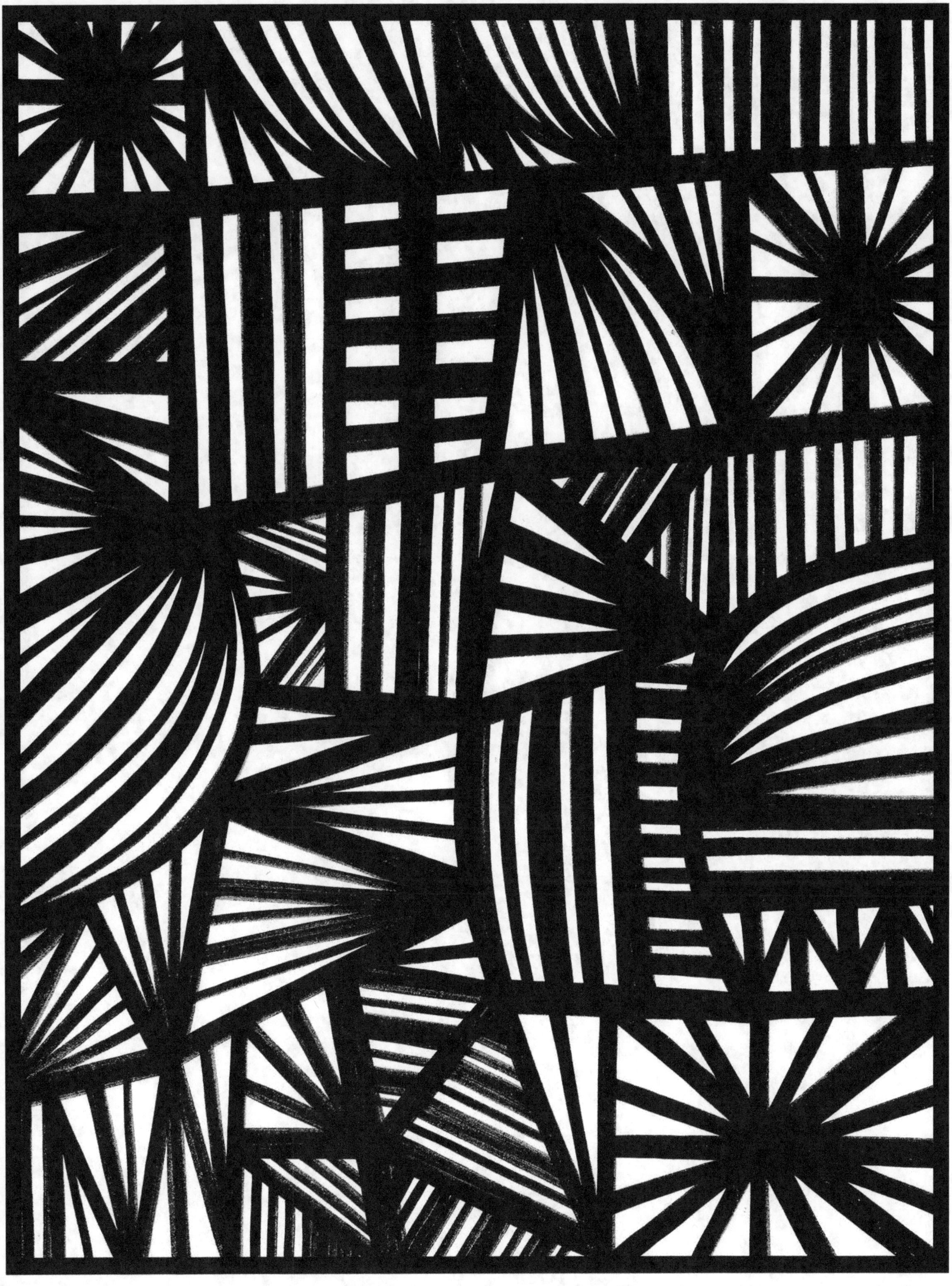

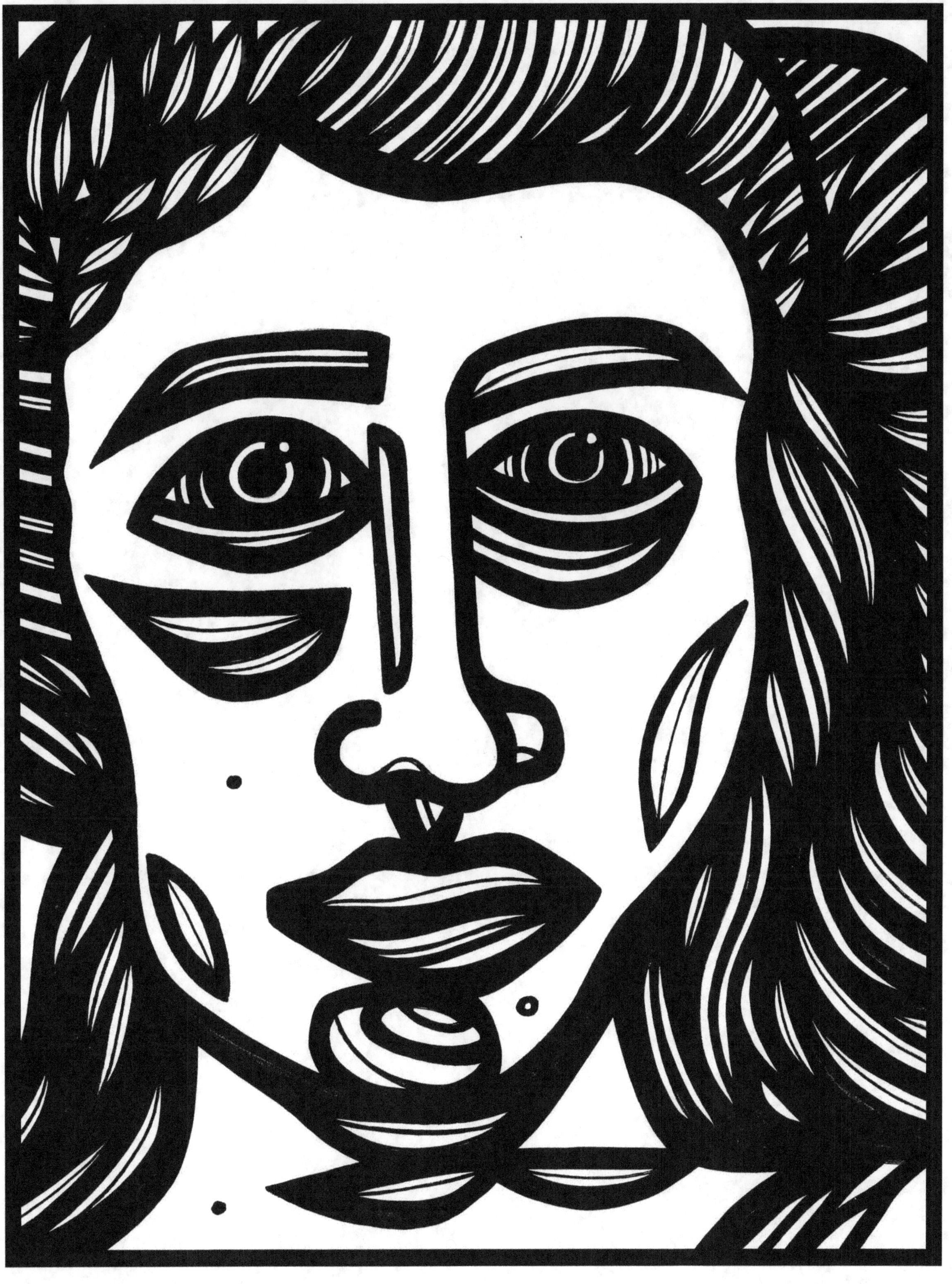

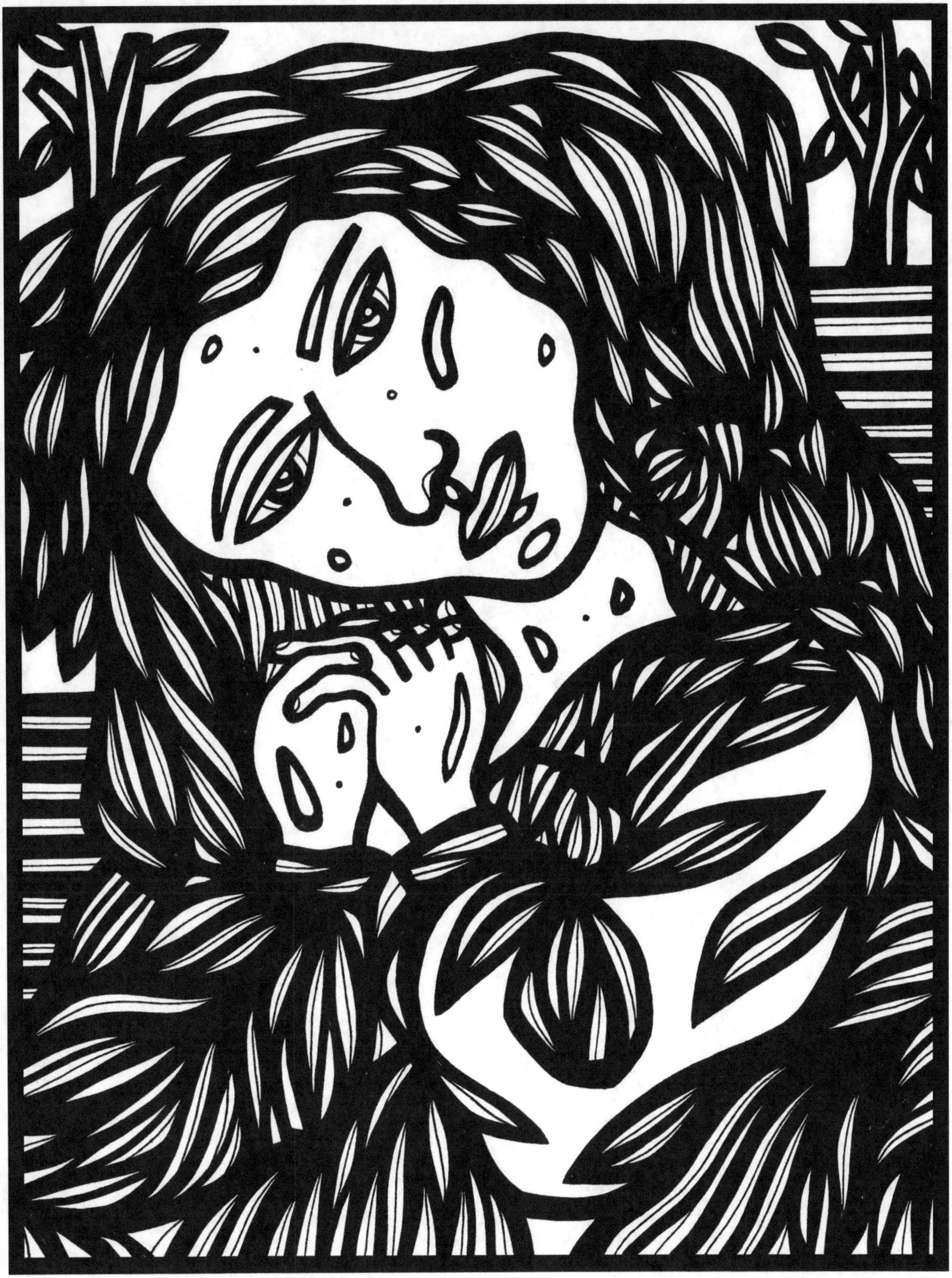

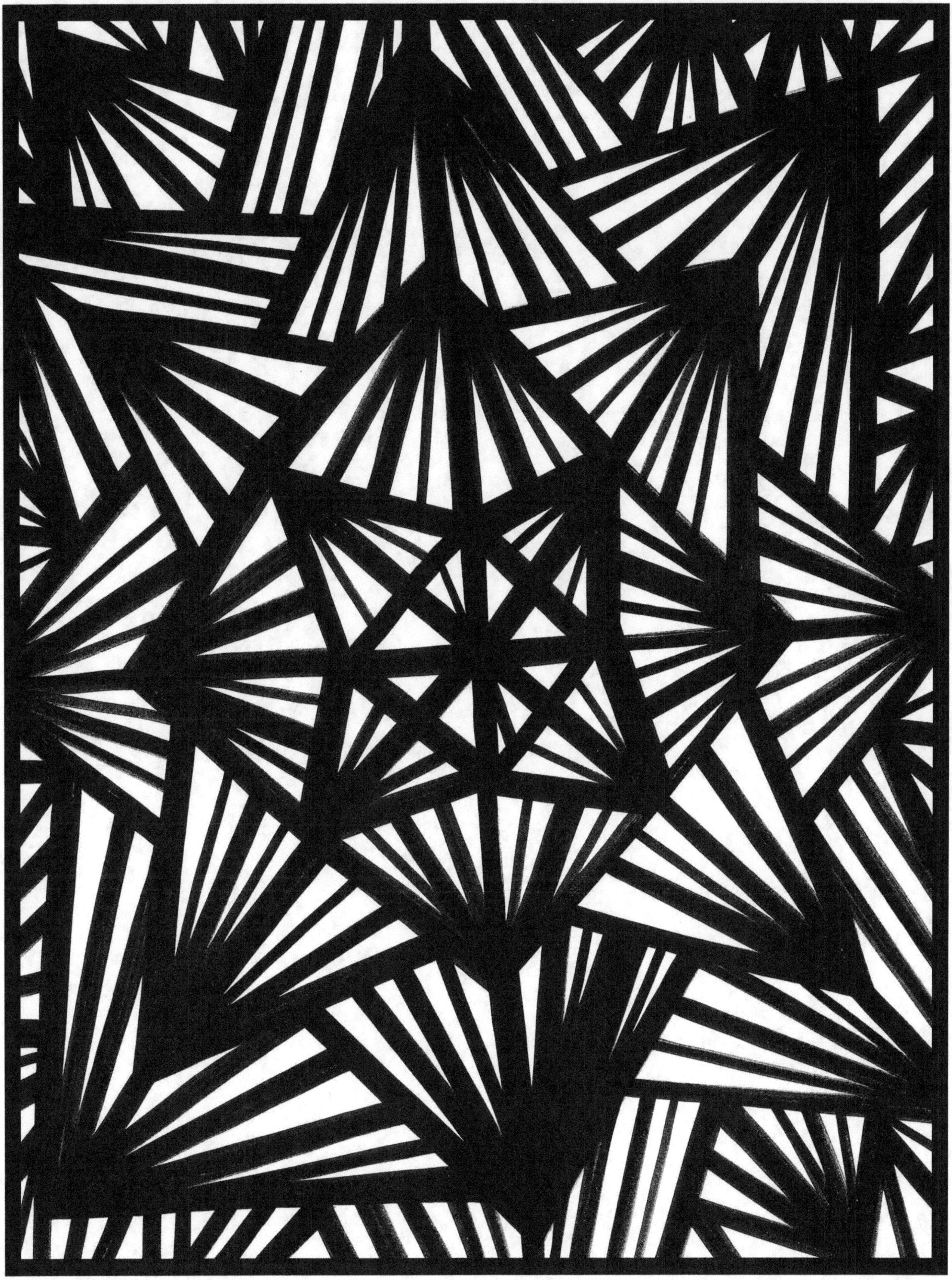

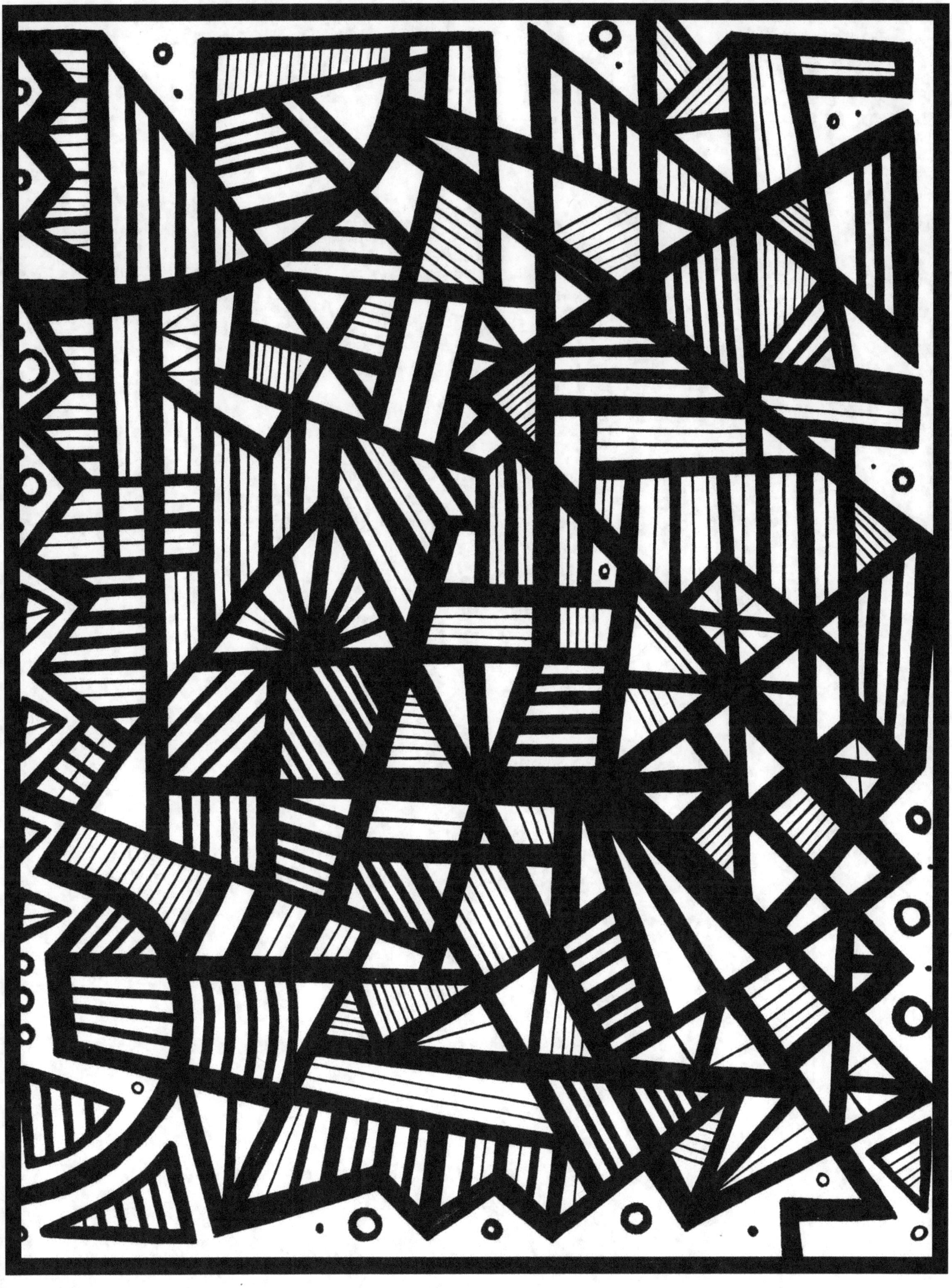

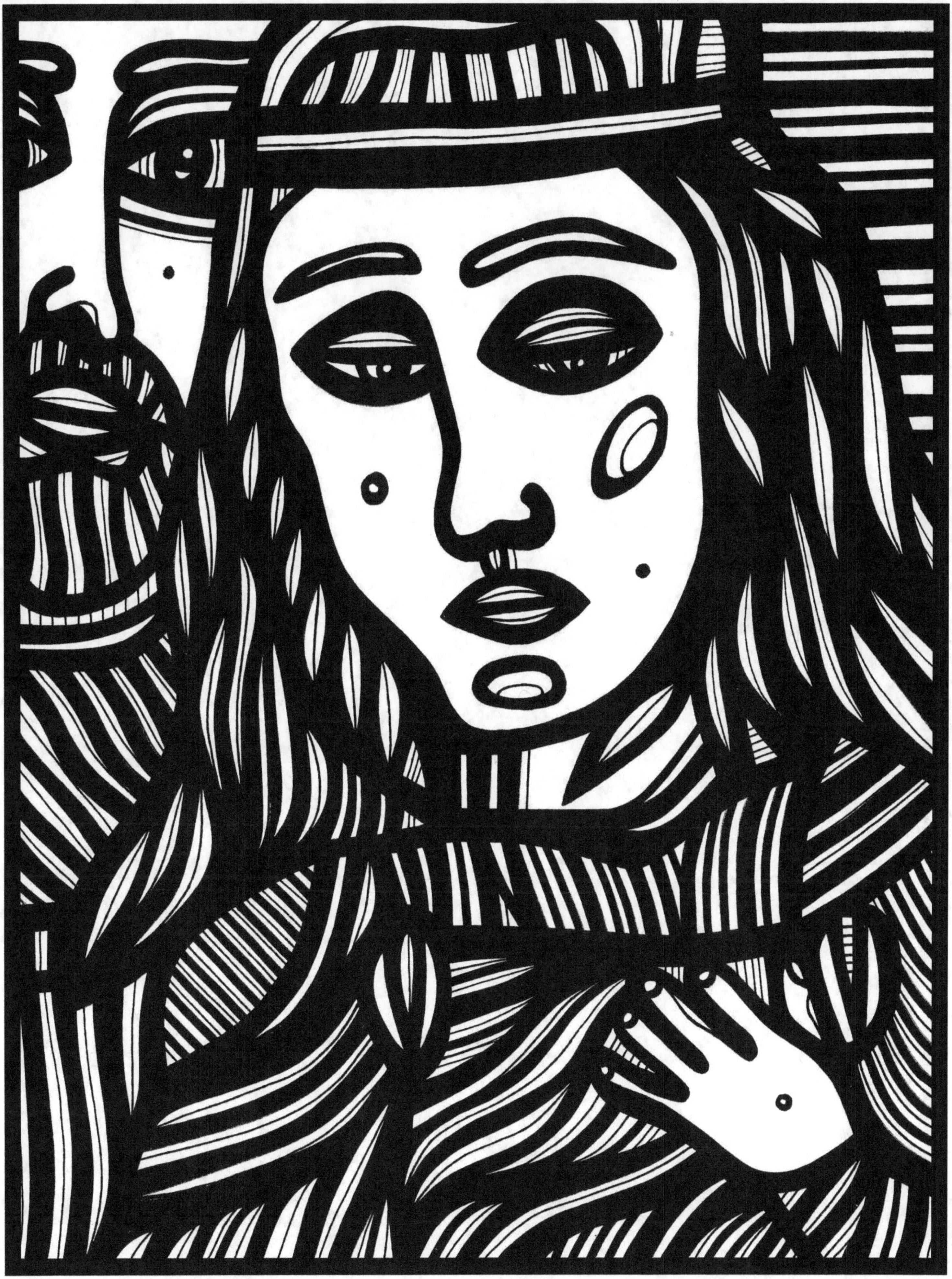

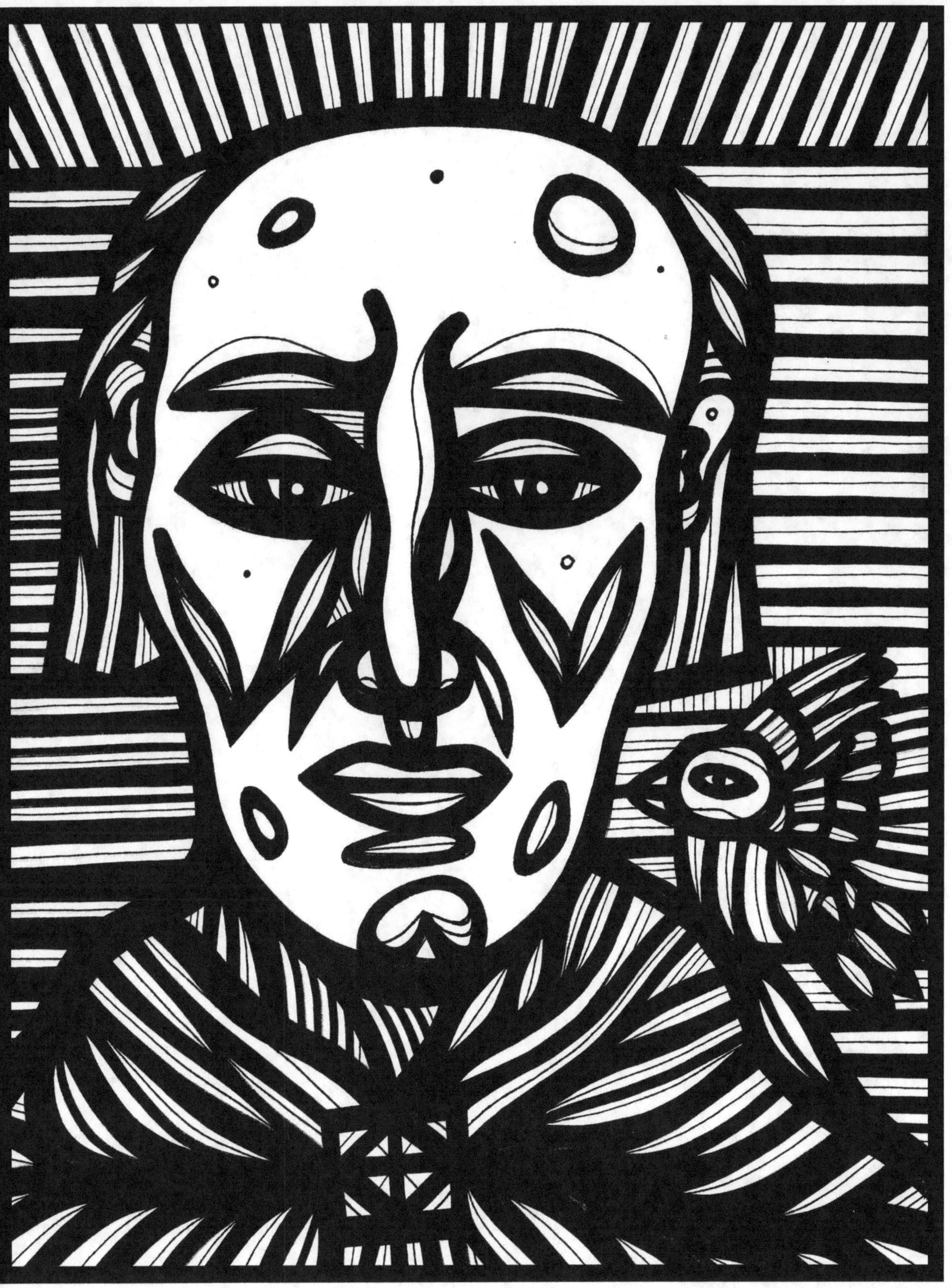

THE END, THANK YOU.

MORE BOOKS:
631ART.COM

www.ingramcontent.com/pod-product-compliance
Lightning Source LLC
Chambersburg PA
CBHW080130240526
45468CB00009BA/2347
9781795671729